Contents

MARCUS CALDWELL

Battles of the Ages

World War II

Introduction

I n the heart of the 20th century, the globe was gripped by a conflict of unparalleled scope and ferocity. The confrontations of the Second World War were more than mere military engagements; they were seismic events that transformed nations, ideologies, and the world's geopolitical landscape. This book seeks to explore these monumental clashes, providing a detailed account of the pivotal battles that came to define this global war.

We trace the roots of conflict from the soft murmurs of discord that swelled into the deafening blasts of war. As the 1930s drew to a close, a world still scarred by the First World War gazed anxiously as storm clouds once again amassed. Nationalistic fervor, the spread of fascism, and imperial ambitions heralded a period of aggressive expansion by the Axis powers, igniting the first sparks of battle and foreshadowing the relentless combat that was yet to unfold.

The swift, brutal campaigns of Blitzkrieg that swept through Poland signaled the war's violent eruption in Europe, while the unforeseen assault on Pearl Harbor dragged the United States into the heart of the conflict. These initial confrontations were not merely displays of force; they were intricate operations marked by strategic foresight, remarkable ingenuity, and the enduring spirit of humanity.

This chronicle is more than a military history; it is a testament to human resilience under the most extreme conditions. It tells the tale of average individuals propelled into the extraordinary vortex of war, often at the cost of everything. The courage, sacrifice, and breakthroughs made during these significant battles form a crucial element of our contemporary heritage.

To fully grasp the magnitude of these battles, one must also understand the backdrop against which they played out. The intricate political schemes, the shifting alliances and hostilities, the decisions of leaders that would determine the fate of millions, and the disrupted lives of civilians are woven into the fabric of this narrative.

This volume serves as a medium for contemplation on the terrors of war, the courage of combatants, the acumen of commanders, and the unexpected outcomes of warfare. It stands as a somber remembrance of the toll of conflict, a homage to the warriors who laid down their lives, and a lesson for the coming generations.

As we commence this historical odyssey, let us honor the courage shown amidst despair and carry forward the teachings imparted by the momentous battles of World War II. Let their remembrance persist as a beacon for harmony and comprehension in a world often fraught with strife and division.

Attack on Pearl Harbor

The potential for conflict between Japan and the United States was recognized by both countries as early as the 1920s. Since the late 1890s, Japan had grown suspicious of U.S. territorial and military activities in the Pacific and Asia, especially with the annexation of regions like Hawaii and the Philippines, which Japan regarded as within or near its sphere of influence.

Japanese strategists also realized the importance of economic self-reliance in modern warfare. Lessons from World War I emphasized that prolonged wars demanded total mobilization and heightened susceptibility to trade embargoes and blockades. This led to Japan's pursuit of vital resources such as iron and oil, which were in limited supply within its own territory.

While Japan's stance toward the U.S. turned sour after the rejection of the Racial Equality Proposal, both nations continued to trade with one another. The real escalation in tensions began with Japan's 1931 invasion of Manchuria. Japan's further incursions into China by 1937 marked the onset of the Second Sino-Japanese War. To sustain their mainland campaign, Japan aimed to sideline China and secure adequate resources independently, with the "Southern Operation" playing a pivotal role in these objectives.

From December 1937 onward, significant events, including the Japanese assault on the USS Panay, the Allison incident, and the Nanking Massacre, greatly shifted Western sentiments against Japan. The U.S., although it considered a blockade of Japan in collaboration with Britain, couldn't see it through. By 1938, under President Roosevelt's guidance, U.S. businesses ceased supplying war tools to Japan.

In 1940, when Japan moved into French Indochina to curb the supplies reaching China, the U.S. responded by withholding deliveries of airplanes, parts, and aviation gasoline to Japan. While this action was perceived as hostile by Japan, the U.S. continued oil exports to prevent extreme provocation due to Japan's heavy reliance on U.S. oil.

In a strategic shift in 1940, President Roosevelt relocated the Pacific Fleet to Hawaii from San Diego and increased military presence in the Philippines. These steps were taken to deter Japanese advances in the East. However, Japan believed that any aggressive move against the UK's Southeast Asian territories would pull the U.S. into the conflict, making a pre-emptive strike crucial to stop American naval involvement. The Philippines, initially to be defended as per the U.S. War Plan Orange, was later deemed indefensible by 1941.

By July 1941, the U.S. cut off oil exports to Japan, primarily after Japan took over French Indochina and due to U.S. domestic oil restrictions. This led Japan to strategize on capturing the oil-abundant Dutch East Indies. Roosevelt warned Japan in August against aggressive actions in "neighboring countries."

Throughout 1941, Japan and the U.S. tried to mend their relations. Japan proposed several concessions, but they were not accepted by Washington. Despite recommendations for a diplomatic meeting, no substantial progress was made. In a final attempt, Japan, in November, proposed conditions that the U.S. found unacceptable. In response, the U.S. issued the Hull note on November 26, demanding Japan's unconditional withdrawal from China.

On the Japanese side, just before receiving the Hull note, they had dispatched a task force towards Pearl Harbor. The intended Pearl Harbor attack aimed to prevent the U.S. Pacific Fleet from obstructing Japan's imminent military actions in Southeast Asia. This move was not only against U.S. territories but also against British and Dutch territories. From Japan's perspective, this attack was essential to act before their resources, particularly oil, depleted.

Early in 1941, Admiral Isoroku Yamamoto, who led Japan's Combined Fleet, initiated preliminary plans to attack Pearl Harbor to safeguard their advancement into the "Southern Resource Area" (Japan's reference to the Dutch East Indies and Southeast Asia). Gaining approval for this plan wasn't straightforward. Yamamoto had to navigate internal disagreements and even threatened to step down from his position. By spring 1941, the planning phase was in full swing, spearheaded by Rear Admiral Ryūnosuke Kusaka with help from Captain Minoru Genda and Captain Kameto Kuroshima, Yamamoto's Deputy Chief of Staff. They meticulously studied the British air assault on the Italian fleet in Taranto that occurred in 1940.

In the following months, pilot training intensified, equipment was optimized, and intelligence gathered. Nonetheless, Emperor Hirohito gave his nod to the attack strategy only on November 5, after several Imperial Conferences. The final green light from the emperor came on December 1, when he was advised that the U.S.'s "Hull Note" would jeopardize Japan's gains in China and threaten their hold over Manchukuo and Korea.

As 1941 neared its end, the possibility of a conflict between the U.S. and Japan loomed large in the public consciousness. A Gallup survey revealed that 52% of Americans anticipated a war with Japan. While the U.S. had frequently placed its Pacific facilities on high alert, officials did not view Pearl Harbor as the likely initial target. Instead, they believed Japan would strike the Philippines first, given its strategic location affecting sea routes and its potential to interrupt Japan's supply chain from the south. U.S. officials also underestimated Japan, believing it couldn't conduct multiple significant naval operations simultaneously.

The Japanese assault on Pearl Harbor was driven by several key objectives.

Primarily, Japan aimed to cripple vital American naval units to prevent the Pacific Fleet from hindering Japan's ambitions in the Dutch East Indies, Malaya, and broader Southeast Asia. This would facilitate a smoother Japanese takeover of these regions. Additionally, Japan sought to gain a strategic advantage by preempting the naval expansion promised by America's 1940 Vinson-Walsh Act. The battleships, being the navy's crown jewels at the time, were specifically targeted to weaken America's power projection in the Pacific. Moreover, Japan believed that such a bold strike would dampen American morale, leading the U.S. to reconsider its stance and potentially negotiate a peace agreement favorable to Japanese interests.

However, attacking the Pacific Fleet while anchored at Pearl Harbor had its drawbacks. The shallow waters meant the damaged ships could potentially be salvaged and repaired. Also, a significant portion of the fleet's crews would likely survive as many were either on shore leave or could be rescued from the harbor. Another critical oversight was the absence of the U.S. Pacific Fleet's three primary aircraft carriers (Enterprise, Lexington, and Saratoga) during the attack. The Japanese naval strategy was heavily influenced by Admiral Mahan's "decisive battle" philosophy, which emphasized the destruction of enemy battleships. Despite these factors, Admiral Yamamoto opted to proceed with the attack.

The Japanese were so confident in securing a swift victory that they overlooked other significant targets in the harbor, such as the navy yard, oil storage facilities, and the submarine base, believing these assets wouldn't impact the short duration of the conflict they anticipated.

On November 26, 1941, a Japanese naval group, labeled the Striking Force, comprised of six aircraft carriers – Akagi, Kaga, Sōryū, Hiryū, Shōkaku, and Zuikaku – set sail from Hittokapu Bay on Etorofu (now Iterup) Island in the Kuril Islands. Their destination was a location northwest of Hawaii, from where they aimed to deploy 408 aircraft against Pearl Harbor. This included 360 aircraft for the primary and secondary waves of attack, and 48 for defense and combat air patrols.

The initial wave was designated as the main assault, with the subsequent wave prioritized to target aircraft carriers first, followed by cruisers, and then battleships. The first wave was equipped mainly with Type 91 aerial torpedoes, which had been modified to function in shallow waters. These aircrews had been instructed to prioritize high-value targets, such as battleships and aircraft carriers. If these weren't available, they were to focus on other significant vessels like cruisers and destroyers. Dive bombers from the first wave had ground installations as their targets. The fighter aircraft were tasked with neutralizing as many stationary aircraft as possible, to minimize the risk of them taking off and confronting the Japanese bombers. Once low on fuel, these fighters would return to their carriers to refuel and rejoin the battle. They were also responsible for providing air cover, particularly over US airstrips.

Before the onslaught began, the Imperial Japanese Navy dispatched reconnaissance planes from the cruisers Chikuma and Tone to survey Oahu and the Lahaina Roads in Maui, respectively. Their mission was to relay information about the composition and positioning of the US fleet. These reconnaissance flights were risky as they could potentially tip off the US. However, they were somewhat redundant as the Japanese already had intelligence from their spy, Takeo Yoshikawa, regarding the US fleet's status and positioning in Pearl Harbor. Information confirming the US fleet's absence from the Lahaina anchorage near Maui was transmitted by the Tone's reconnaissance aircraft and the submarine I-72. Additionally, four other scout planes were tasked with monitoring the area between the Japanese carrier group and Niihau Island, to detect potential counterattacks.

A group of fleet submarines, namely I-16, I-18, I-20, I-22, and I-24, transported a Type A midget submarine each to the vicinity of Oahu. Setting sail from Kure Naval District on November 25, 1941, they approached within 10 nmi of Pearl Harbor's entrance by December 6. On the early hours of

December 7, they released their midget subs. Minesweeper Condor detected one midget submarine's periscope and informed destroyer Ward, which later sank a different midget sub. Another midget submarine missed its targets near Ford Island and was eventually destroyed by destroyer Monaghan.

A third midget sub, Ha-19, got stranded twice and was eventually captured on December 8. Its pilot, Ensign Kazuo Sakamaki, was taken prisoner, marking the first Japanese POW capture. Another midget sub was damaged and discarded by its crew, only to be discovered in 1960. Interestingly, a radio transmission from a midget submarine on December 8 reported damages to significant warships inside the harbor.

Decades later, in 1992, 2000, and 2001, underwater research located the remnants of the fifth midget submarine outside Pearl Harbor. Both its torpedoes were missing, aligning with claims of torpedoes launched at the light cruiser St. Louis and possibly the destroyer Helm. However, the St. Louis' reported torpedo might have been a minesweeping float from the destroyer Boggs. A photograph from the 1941 Pearl Harbor attack, which was released to the public in the 2000s, reportedly indicates the fifth midget submarine launching torpedoes at the battleships West Virginia and Oklahoma. Given the size of these torpedoes, some speculate they played a significant role in the severe damages and the capsizing of Oklahoma. Admiral Chester Nimitz reported to Congress about recovering a large, unexploded torpedo in the harbor, suggesting it was bigger than the aerial ones.

The assault occurred without an official war declaration from Japan, contrary to Admiral Yamamoto's plan. He had specified that the offensive should only start thirty minutes after Japan notified the US that peace talks had ceased. Nonetheless, the onset of the attack preceded this notification. Tokyo sent the lengthy "14-Part Message" to their Washington Embassy, but due to its length, the Japanese ambassador couldn't present it until after the attack had started. Interestingly, US cryptanalysts had already decoded most of this message ahead of its intended delivery time. This message, although hinting at an end to negotiations and possible war, neither declared war nor ended diplomatic ties. While Japan's newspapers heralded a war declaration on December 8, the US government received it only post-attack.

For many years, it was believed that Japan's failure to formally end diplomatic ties before the attack was due to unintended delays in delivering their message to Washington.

The initial wave of 183 Japanese aircraft, spearheaded by Commander Mitsuo Fuchida, took off towards Oahu from north of the island. Six planes couldn't be dispatched due to technical issues.

Upon nearing Oahu, the U.S. Army's SCR-270 radar system at Opana Point on the northern end of the island detected them. Although this radar station had been training for some time, it was not fully operational. Operators, Privates George Elliot Jr. and Joseph Lockard, relayed their findings to Private Joseph P. McDonald at Fort Shafter's Intercept Center near Pearl Harbor. However, Lieutenant Kermit A. Tyler, an officer at the Intercept Center, mistakenly believed it was a scheduled group of six B-17 bombers from California. Since the incoming Japanese aircraft and the B-17s were approaching from nearly the same direction, and the radar operators hadn't witnessed such a large formation previously, they failed to communicate its magnitude to Tyler. Tyler, bound by security protocols, did not inform the operators about the expected B-17s, even though this wasn't classified.

As the Japanese planes neared Oahu, they intercepted and downed several U.S. planes. One of them managed to send out a garbled warning. Yet, other alerts from vessels outside the harbor were still being evaluated or awaited confirmation when the air raid started at 7:48 a.m. Hawaiian Time. The first target was Kaneohe. In total, 353 Japanese aircraft attacked in two phases. The first wave, led by slower torpedo bombers, focused on the primary ships, particularly the battleships. Simultaneously, dive bombers struck U.S. airfields on Oahu, prioritizing Hickam Field and Wheeler Field. The subsequent wave of 171 planes targeted Bellows Field near Kaneohe and Ford Island. The only air resistance they faced came from a few P-36 Hawks, P-40 Warhawks, and some SBD Dauntless dive bombers from the carrier, Enterprise.

During the initial wave of the assault, approximately eight of the forty-nine armor-piercing bombs, each weighing 1760 lb, accurately struck battleship targets. Some of these bombs malfunctioned upon impact, while others didn't penetrate unarmored decks as intended. Of the forty torpedoes launched, thirteen targeted and hit battleships, with four impacting other vessels.

US ship crew members were jolted awake by the cacophony of alarms, explosions, and gunfire. In their disoriented state, they hastily donned their uniforms and rushed to their battle stations. The urgent communication, "Air raid Pearl Harbor. This is not drill.", originated from Patrol Wing Two's headquarters, making it the earliest Hawaiian senior command to react. The American forces were taken by surprise. Key ammunition storage was locked, aircraft were positioned closely together in the open to prevent potential sabotage, and many gun stations were unmanned. In fact, none of the Navy's primary 5"/38 guns, only a fraction of its machine guns, and a mere four out of 31 Army batteries were operational.

Nevertheless, despite the apparent unpreparedness, numerous American military members showcased commendable resilience and quick response. Ensign Joseph Taussig Jr., stationed on the Nevada, managed the ship's anti-aircraft guns and, even after being gravely injured, continued his duties. In the absence of its captain, Lieutenant Commander F. J. Thomas steered the Nevada until it ran aground at 9:10 a.m. The destroyer Aylwin, interestingly, set sail with just four junior officers on board and remained at sea for over a day before its commanding officer rejoined. Captain Mervyn Bennion, leading the West Virginia, courageously directed his crew until he was fatally injured by bomb shrapnel from the neighboring Tennessee.

The subsequent wave planned to deploy 171 aircraft: 54 B5Ns, 81 D3As, and 36 A6Ms, under the leadership of Lieutenant-Commander Shigekazu Shimazaki. Four aircraft couldn't take off due to technical issues.

This second wave was split into three units. One unit was designated to target Kāne'ohe, while the others focused on Pearl Harbor itself. These units converged on their target locations nearly simultaneously from various routes.

The assault ended 90 minutes after it started. During that time, 2,008 sailors lost their lives and another 710 were injured. 218 soldiers and airmen, who were once part of the Army before the US Air Force became independent in 1947, were killed, with 364 wounded. 109 Marines died and another 69 were injured. 68 civilians also lost their lives, with 35 wounded. Altogether, 2,403 Americans died and 1,178 were injured. Eighteen ships, including five battleships, were either sunk or beached. All Americans harmed in this attack were technically non-combatants since the assault happened during a time of peace.

About half of the American deaths resulted from the explosion in the Arizona's front magazine after being struck by a modified 16-inch shell. Craig Nelson, an author, mentioned that most of the US sailors who perished at Pearl Harbor were lower-ranking crew members. He noted that most Navy officers resided in houses, so it was primarily the young sailors on the ships who faced the brunt of the attack. These sailors were typically around 17 or 18 years old.

Notably, nine civilian firefighters from the Honolulu Fire Department who went to assist at Hickam Field during the attack were harmed. They are recognized as the only fire department members on US soil ever attacked by a foreign entity. Fireman Harry Tuck Lee Pang from Engine 6 was shot near the hangars by a Japanese plane. Captains Thomas Macy and John Carreira of Engine 4 and Engine 1, respectively, lost their lives inside a hangar following a bomb drop. Six more firefighters suffered injuries due to Japanese shrapnel.

These injured firefighters were awarded Purple Hearts on June 13, 1944, for their courageous actions during peacetime. However, the three deceased firefighters only received their Purple Hearts on the 43rd anniversary of the attack, December 7, 1984. These nine individuals remain the sole non-military firefighters in US history to earn this honor.

The Nevada, already impaired by a torpedo and aflame, tried to leave the harbor. As she moved, Japanese bombers targeted her, inflicting further damage and igniting more fires. To prevent blocking the harbor's entrance, she was intentionally run aground. California took hits from two bombs and two torpedoes. While her crew could potentially have kept her afloat, they were directed to desert the ship during an effort to activate the pumps. Flames and oil from the Arizona and West Virginia exacerbated the scene. The unarmed Utah was struck by two torpedoes, while West Virginia was hit by seven, with the final one damaging her rudder. Four torpedoes hit Oklahoma, causing her to overturn. Maryland was struck by two modified 16" shells, causing minimal damage.

Though the Japanese focused on battleships, they didn't neglect other ships. The light cruiser Helena was hit by a torpedo, causing the nearby minelayer Oglala to overturn from the resulting shockwave. In dry dock, destroyers Cassin and Downes were wrecked by bombs that ignited their fuel. The consequential fire, combined with flooding attempts, devastated both ships. Cassin was displaced from her supports and collided with Downes. Light cruisers Raleigh and Honolulu were also hit, with Raleigh taking a torpedo strike. The repair ship Vestal, adjacent to Arizona, suffered heavy damage and was grounded. Seaplane tender Curtiss and destroyer Shaw faced significant damages too.

Out of 402 American aircraft in Hawaii, 188 were decimated and 159 harmed, with 155 on land. Virtually none were combat-ready. Eight Army Air Forces pilots took to the skies during the attack, with six pilots credited for downing Japanese aircraft: Lieutenants Sanders, Rasmussen, Taylor, Welch, Brown, and Sterling Jr. 30 out of 33 PBYs stationed in Hawaii were obliterated, while three on duty remained unscathed. Some U.S. planes, including four from an incoming flight from Enterprise, were mistakenly shot down by friendly fire.

During the assault, nine civilian planes were in the air around Pearl Harbor; three were downed by the Japanese.

In the assault, Japan lost 55 airmen and nine submariners, with Kazuo Saka-maki being captured. Out of Japan's 414 operational planes, 350 participated in the attack. They lost 29 aircraft: nine in the initial assault (three fighters, one dive bomber, and five torpedo bombers) and 20 in the subsequent wave (six fighters and fourteen dive bombers). Additionally, ground-based anti aircraft fire damaged another 74 aircraft.

Some narratives suggest that various Japanese junior officers, including Fuchida and Genda, pressed Nagumo to initiate a third strike to further decimate Pearl Harbor's remaining naval assets and impair its drydock facilities, maintenance shops, and oil storage areas. Fuchida has detailed this meeting post-war on multiple occasions. Yet, some historians question the authenticity of Fuchida's recollections, as they sometimes diverge from established historical records. Genda, who during the attack's planning believed three strikes were essential to incapacitate the Pacific Fleet, refuted claims that he advocated for a subsequent assault.

While a potential third strike would likely have concentrated on the base's leftover ships, many military historians posit that any significant destruction to the onshore infrastructures would have severely impeded the US Pacific Fleet's operations. Admiral Chester W. Nimitz, who later led the Pacific Fleet, estimated that it could have extended the war by another two years.

In a meeting on his flagship the next day, Yamamoto concurred with Nagumo's choice to retreat without deploying a third wave. In hindsight, leaving the crucial dockyards, maintenance shops, and oil storage intact enabled the US to promptly counteract Japanese maneuvers in the Pacific. Yamamoto eventually expressed regret over Nagumo's decision, firmly believing that omitting a third strike was a significant oversight.

Following a thorough search for survivors, Captain Homer N. Wallin was tasked with overseeing an official salvage mission.

In and around Pearl Harbor, a collaboration of Navy divers, personnel from the Pearl Harbor Naval Shipyard, and civilian workers from companies like the Pacific Bridge Company initiated salvage efforts on ships that were viable for refloating. Their tasks included patching up damages, removing debris, and draining water from the vessels. Navy divers specifically undertook operations within the compromised ships. In a span of six months, five battleships and two cruisers were mended or refloated, enabling them to be transported to shipyards both in Pearl Harbor and the mainland for comprehensive repairs.

Salvage endeavors persisted rigorously for an additional year, amounting to roughly 20,000 hours of underwater work. Both the Arizona and the target ship Utah were beyond the scope of salvage and were left submerged, with the Arizona later becoming a war memorial. The Oklahoma was successfully raised but never underwent repairs and tragically overturned en route to the mainland in 1947. Salvaging and restoring the Nevada presented numerous challenges; tragically, two individuals involved in the process perished after inhaling toxic gases inside the ship. Whenever possible, weapons and equipment were extracted from irreparably damaged ships and repurposed for other vessels.

The day following the assault, Roosevelt addressed Congress with his renowned Day of Infamy speech, urging for an official war declaration against Japan. Congress rapidly responded, endorsing his appeal in less than an hour. On December 11, Germany and Italy, despite not being obliged by the Tripartite Pact, declared war on the United States. That same day, Congress reciprocated by declaring war on both Germany and Italy.

Britain had already been engaged in war against Germany since September 1939 and Italy since June 1940. British Prime Minister Winston Churchill had earlier pledged to declare war on Japan immediately if it attacked the US. When Churchill became aware of Japan's offensives against Malaya, Singapore, and Hong Kong, he deemed it unnecessary to delay or consult with the US any further. He swiftly summoned the Japanese Ambassador, leading the UK to declare war on Japan a full nine hours ahead of the US.

The assault deeply rattled all Allied forces in the Pacific. This initial setback was intensified by subsequent defeats. Mere hours after the Pearl Harbor attack, Japan launched an assault on the Philippines. Just three days post-Pearl Harbor, the Prince of Wales battleship and the Repulse battlecruiser were destroyed off Malaya's coast.

During the war, Pearl Harbor was a recurring theme in U.S. propaganda.

Another outcome of the Pearl Harbor attack, especially highlighted by events like the Niihau incident, was the relocation of Japanese-American residents and citizens to internment camps. Soon after the attack, several Japanese-American leaders were detained and sent to high-security locations such as Sand Island near Honolulu and the Kilauea Military Camp on Hawaii's island. While over 110,000 Japanese Americans from the West Coast were relocated to these camps, in Hawaii, which had a significant Japanese American population constituting over a third of its residents, only 1,200 to 1,800 were interned.

Internationally, the attack had repercussions as well. British Columbia in Canada, with its significant Japanese immigrant population, experienced heightened tensions following Pearl Harbor. This led the Canadian government to act decisively. On February 24, 1942, under the War Measures Act, Order-in-Council P.C. no. 1486 was enacted. This order mandated the forcible relocation of all Japanese Canadians in British Columbia and barred their return. By March 4, policies were in place to carry out these evacuations. Consequently, 12,000 Japanese Canadians were interned, 2,000 were assigned to road camps, and another 2,000 were made to work on sugar beet farms in the prairies.

In recognition of the valor displayed during the attack, 15 Medals of Honor, 51 Navy Crosses, 53 Silver Stars, four Navy and Marine Corps Medals, one Distinguished Flying Cross, four Distinguished Service Crosses, one Distinguished Service Medal, and three Bronze Stars were conferred upon American servicemen at Pearl Harbor. Later, the Pearl Harbor Commemorative Medal was introduced to honor all military veterans of the attack.

The planners behind the Pearl Harbor attack recognized the need for a rescue location for pilots whose aircraft were too damaged to make it back to their carriers. They selected the island of Niihau, a mere thirty-minute flight from Pearl Harbor, as this safe haven.

During the attack's second wave, Petty Officer Shigenori Nishikaichi's Zero fighter from the Hiryu was damaged during his raid on Wheeler. He proceeded to land on Niihau, but his aircraft sustained more damage upon crash landing. One of the Native Hawaiians on the island assisted Nishikaichi out of his damaged plane and, sensing the strained relations between the U.S. and Japan, confiscated the pilot's pistol, maps, codes, and other essential documents. The inhabitants of Niihau were isolated, with no phones or radios, and thus, had no knowledge of the Pearl Harbor attack. Seeking to retrieve his documents, Nishikaichi sought the aid of three Japanese American residents on the island. In the resulting confrontations, Nishikaichi lost his life, a Hawaiian civilian was injured, one of the Japanese American helpers took their own life, while his wife and another accomplice were incarcerated.

The apparent readiness of the local Japanese residents to assist Nishikaichi raised alarms and further fueled suspicions that local Japanese Americans might be disloyal.

The attack on Pearl Harbor achieved its immediate objective, but in the grander scheme, it seemed somewhat redundant. Unknown to Yamamoto, the mastermind behind the assault, the U.S. Navy had decided as early as 1935 not to make a rapid Pacific advance toward the Philippines should war break out, as part of the evolution of Plan Orange. Instead, by 1940, the U.S. had embraced "Plan Dog," prioritizing keeping the Imperial Japanese Navy away from the eastern Pacific and the vital shipping routes to Australia while focusing on neutralizing Nazi Germany.

A saving grace for the U.S. was that its aircraft carriers remained unscathed. Had they been damaged, the Pacific Fleet's offensive capacity would have been hindered for a significant period, assuming no support from the Atlantic Fleet. In the aftermath of the attack, the U.S. Navy's strategy hinged on carriers and submarines—the very instruments that played a pivotal role in halting and then pushing back the Japanese progression. Though six of the eight battleships at Pearl Harbor were eventually refurbished and redeployed, their limitations in speed and high fuel use restricted their roles, mainly to shore bombardments. The Japanese, influenced by Captain Alfred Thayer Mahan's doctrine, erroneously believed that battleships would dictate the ultimate Pacific conflict. Consequently, Yamamoto and those after him preserved battleships for a "decisive battle" that never materialized.

Japan's overconfidence in securing a swift victory led them to overlook key targets at Pearl Harbor, including navy repair yards, oil storage facilities, the submarine base, and the old headquarters. Despite their significance, these facilities were omitted from Genda's target list. Their preservation was crucial to the U.S. Pacific war effort. Maintaining these assets ensured that Pearl Harbor could provide essential logistical support for pivotal operations, including the Doolittle Raid and the Battles of the Coral Sea and Midway. U.S. submarines, in particular, played a significant role in stymying the IJN and crippling Japan's economy by severely restricting its import capabilities. By the close of 1942, Japan's raw material imports had dwindled dramatically, and oil imports had nearly halted. Furthermore, the Old Administration Building's basement housed a cryptanalytic unit that played an instrumental role in several American naval victories, including the Battle of Midway.

Battle of Wake Island

I n January 1941, the U.S. Navy established a military outpost on the atoll. On 19 August, the inaugural permanent military garrison, components of the 1st Marine Defense Battalion, arrived at Wake Island. They were led by Major P.S. Devereux, USMC, and comprised 450 officers and personnel. Given the atoll's compact size, the Marines couldn't staff all defensive posts, and they were without some essential equipment, notably their air search radar units. Enhancing the Marine Detachment was the Marine Corps Fighter Squadron VMF-211, with 12 F4F-3 Wildcat fighters, under the leadership of Major Paul A. Putnam, USMC. The island also hosted 68 U.S. Navy members and approximately 1,221 civilian workers from the Morrison-Knudsen Civil Engineering Company, responsible for construction projects on the island. Many of these workers had previously been engaged in significant construction endeavors like the Boulder Dam, Bonneville Dam, and Grand Coulee Dam projects. Others joined due to challenging circumstances and a pressing need for income. Additionally, 45 Chamorro men (indigenous Micronesians from the Mariana Islands and Guam) worked for Pan American Airways at the island's facilities, servicing the Pan Am Clipper trans-Pacific amphibious air route established in 1935.

The Marines had an arsenal that included six 5-inch guns from the old battle-ship USS Texas, twelve 3 in anti-aircraft weapons (but only one functional anti-aircraft director among them), eighteen .50 in Browning heavy machine guns, and thirty .30 in various machine guns, both water- and air-cooled.

On 28 November, naval pilot Commander Winfield S. Cunningham, USN, arrived at Wake Island to take charge of the U.S. forces stationed there. He had a mere 10 days to inspect the defenses and evaluate his troops before hostilities began.

By 6 December, the Japanese Submarine Division 27, consisting of Ro-65, Ro-66, and Ro-67, set out from Kwajalein Atoll, with a mission to patrol and set a blockade for the forthcoming operation.

December 7 dawned clear and bright over Wake Island. Just a day before, Major Devereux had organized a drill for his Marines - notably the first, as priority had been given to fortifying the island's defenses.

On 8 December, a mere few hours after learning about the attack on Pearl Harbor (due to Wake's location on the other side of the International Date Line), 36 Japanese Mitsubishi G3M3 medium bombers, originating from the Marshall Islands, launched an assault on Wake Island. This attack destroyed eight out of the 12 F4F-3 Wildcats stationed there and sank the Nisqually, a former cargo ship repurposed into a scow. Four of the Wildcats were in mid-air patrol during the raid. Poor visibility prevented them from spotting the incoming Japanese bombers. However, these airborne Wildcats managed to shoot down two bombers the next day. The marine base's defensive positions were unharmed in the raid, which mostly aimed at the aircraft. Out of the Marine aviation personnel, 23 lost their lives, and 11 sustained injuries.

Post this assault, Pan Am workers, along with passengers of the Philippine Clipper – a Martin 130 amphibious aircraft that evaded damage during the attack – were evacuated. However, the Chamorro workers were not permitted to board the aircraft and were left stranded.

Subsequently, two more aerial attacks took place. The primary base was hit on 9 December, leading to the destruction of both the civilian hospital and the Pan Am facilities. Enemy bombardment the next day was concentrated on the distant Wilkes Island. After the 9 December strike, to trick any Japanese surveillance, the four anti-aircraft guns were relocated and wooden fakes were set up in their previous locations. Japanese bombers, deceived, targeted these dummy positions. A fortunate hit on a civilian dynamite stash initiated a domino effect, annihilating the ammunition meant for the guns on Wilkes.

In the early hours of 11 December, the defenders, aided by the four remaining Wildcats, thwarted the initial Japanese landing led by the South Seas Force. This force consisted of light cruisers Yubari, Tenryū, and Tatsuta; older Mutsuki and Kamikaze-class destroyers such as Yayoi, Mutsuki, Kisaragi, Hayate, Mochizuki, and Oite; submarine tender Jingei, two merchantmen with armaments (Kinryu Maru and Kongō Maru), and two patrol boats retrofitted in 1941 to deploy a landing craft via a stern ramp, which held 450 Special Naval Landing Force troops. Nearby, submarines Ro-65, Ro-66, and Ro-67 secured the perimeter.

The US Marines engaged the approaching fleet with their six 5-inch coast-defense guns. Major Devereux, leading the Marines under Cunningham, instructed gunners to withhold their fire until adversaries were within the coastal defenses' reach. From Peale islet, "Battery L" struck Hayate from approximately 4,000 yards, landing at least two hits on her ammunition storage. This caused a massive explosion, sinking the ship in under two minutes, witnessed by the shoreline defenders. Although Battery A reported hitting Yubari multiple times, her operational log didn't note any inflicted damage. Furthermore, the Wildcats managed to sink destroyer Kisaragi by bombing her stern, where depth charges were stored. This resulted in the loss of two destroyers with Hayate being the first Japanese naval vessel sunk in the conflict. The Japanese reported 407 losses in this initial attempt and withdrew without making a landing, marking their first reversal against the Americans.

Following this successful defense, US media claimed Commander Cunningham, when asked about reinforcements and supplies, humorously replied,

"Send us more Japs!" In reality, Cunningham dispatched a detailed list of essential equipment, such as gunsights, spare components, and fire-control radar, to his immediate supervisor at the 14th Naval District. However, the Americans remained under siege, facing regular Japanese aerial assaults without any reinforcements or supplies.

Admiral Fletcher's Task Force 14 (TF–14) was given the mission to relieve Wake Island, while Admiral Brown's Task Force 11 was assigned to stage a diversionary raid on Jaluit in the Marshall Islands. Another task force, led by Vice Admiral Halsey and centered on the Enterprise, was designated to provide support, especially since the Japanese Second Carrier Division posed a considerable threat in the operational vicinity.

TF–14's fleet comprised the carrier Saratoga, oiler Neches, seaplane tender Tangier, three heavy cruisers (Astoria, Minneapolis, and San Francisco), and eight destroyers (Selfridge, Mugford, Jarvis, Patterson, Ralph Talbot, Henley, Blue, and Helm). This convoy was equipped with the 4th Marine Defense Battalion, the VMF-221 fighter squadron with Brewster F2A-3 Buffalo fighters, along with substantial equipment and ammunition supplies. They carried gear for 3-inch AA batteries, spare parts for 5-inch defense guns, thousands of rounds of ammunition, machine gun teams, and radar equipment, among others.

Meanwhile, TF–11 was composed of the carrier Lexington, oiler Neosho, three heavy cruisers (Indianapolis, Chicago, and Portland), and nine destroyers from Destroyer Squadron 1, with Phelps as the flagship.

On the night of 22 December, after obtaining intelligence about the presence of two IJN carriers and what were believed to be two fast battleships near Wake Island, Vice Admiral William S. Pye, who was the interim Commander in Chief of the U.S. Pacific Fleet, directed TF 14 to revert to Pearl Harbor.

The initial defense by the garrison drew the attention of the Japanese Navy, prompting them to send reinforcements. Fresh from their Pearl Harbor assault, the Second Carrier Division (comprising Sōryū and Hiryū) and several other divisions and ships from different missions joined to bolster the attack on Wake Island.

On 23 December, the reinforced Japanese forces, numbering around 1,500 marines, launched their second invasion attempt. Following an intense bombardment, they began their land assault at multiple points on the atoll. They encountered fierce resistance from Lieutenant Robert Hanna and his "3" inch gun, which took out two ex-destroyers. As the Japanese marines proceeded inland, they faced a spirited counterattack led by Captain Platt, pushing them back. However, after relentless combat, the American defenders, heavily outnumbered, were eventually overwhelmed.

During the 15-day standoff, the US Marines suffered 49 fatalities, two went missing, and 49 were wounded. Additionally, at least 70 US civilians, including 10 Chamorros, were killed. A total of 433 US personnel, mainly civilian contractors from Morrison-Knudsen Company, were taken prisoner.

The Japanese reported 144 casualties, including losses from the SNLF and Army, and losses on their ships. Their aircraft losses were also significant, with at least 28 being shot down or damaged.

Captain Henry T. Elrod displayed remarkable heroism during the siege, for which he was posthumously awarded the Medal of Honor. His feats included downing two Japanese G3M Nells aircraft, sinking the destroyer Kisaragi, and leading ground defenses after US aircraft were rendered non-operational. To honor the valiant defenders of Wake Island, a unique military decoration, the Wake Island Device, was introduced.

Lieut. Col. Walter Bayler was the lone Marine from Wake Island to evade capture or death. Departing via a US Navy PBY Catalina on 20 December, Bayler was vital in communicating the events on Wake Island to the American public, even featuring in a nationwide magazine. As a radio technician, Bayler's expertise was deemed crucial elsewhere, which led to his departure on the only available aircraft.

Two U.S. submarines of the Tambor-class patrolled the waters near Wake, while the Japanese had at least six submarines in the vicinity. Interestingly, the Japanese lost two of their submarines during the operation, but not directly due to enemy confrontations. One mishap occurred when two submarines collided with each other, and another Japanese submarine ran aground on a reef while attempting to return to its base. The U.S. submarine did engage a Japanese vessel, but without any discernible impact.

Before the conflict began, the USS Triton and the USS Tambor, two USN submarines, patrolled the waters near Wake. One crew member of the USS Triton fell ill and was transported to Wake Island on December 1, 1941. This individual was taken as a prisoner of war but survived World War II.

The Triton, as a part of Submarine Division 62, embarked on a training expedition to Midway between August 30 and September 15, later joining local and fleet activities around Hawaii. On November 19, the submarine ventured west for a mock war patrol, reaching the vicinity of Wake Island on November 26. On December 8, the Triton noticed smoke columns above the island, mistaking it for onshore construction activity. That evening, upon surfacing to recharge her batteries, the Triton received a radio message informing her of the attack on Pearl Harbor and was directed to keep a safe distance from Wake's defenses. The subsequent day, the Triton witnessed the Japanese assault on the island. On the night of December 10, while surfaced and recharging, the submarine spotted an enemy vessel in the moonlight. Immediately diving deep, the Triton dodged the enemy and, using sonar data, released the first four American torpedoes of World War II. An explosion was heard, but no sinking was confirmed, and the Triton did not receive credit for a hit. Despite the Japanese deploying the aircraft carriers Hiryū and Sōryū after their initial setback on December 11, the Triton remained uninformed and did not challenge them. The submarine also did not attempt any evacuations from Wake. On December 21, she was instructed to head back to Hawaii, docking in Pearl Harbor on the last day of the year.

The USS Tambor, facing mechanical issues, had to make its way back to Hawaii in mid-December and did not partake in any combat actions.

On December 6, 1941, the Ro-66 embarked from Kwajalein, carrying the commander of Submarine Squadron 27, to survey Wake Island. The Japanese had plans to invade it on December 8, which marked the commencement of the Battle of Wake Island. The Ro-65, Ro-66, and Ro-67 were in the vicinity, backing the Japanese in their endeavor to capture the atoll. On December 11, US Marine Corps troops on Wake repelled the initial Japanese invasion.

As the Japanese readied more troops for another larger invasion, on December 12, Submarine Squadron 7 instructed all Submarine Division 27 submarines to head back to Kwajalein. While Ro-65 and Ro-67 made their way back, Ro-66, due to a radio malfunction, didn't receive the order. Thus, she continued patrolling off Wake Island, even as the Ro-60, Ro-61, and Ro-62 from Submarine Division 26 came to replace the original trio.

On December 17, before dawn, Ro-66 was on the surface near Wake Island, charging her batteries amidst a heavy squall when Ro-62, also on the surface, appeared. Both tried to avoid each other, but a collision was inevitable. Ro-62 struck Ro-66, causing her to sink and resulting in the loss of 63 lives, including the Submarine Division 27 commander. Only three crew members from Ro-66, thrown overboard by the collision, were saved by Ro-62.

The Ro-60, with Ro-61 and Ro-62, were at Kwajalein during Japan's entry into WWII on December 8, Kwajalein time. They were put on "standby alert" that day, given the US Marine Corps' success in fending off Japan's first invasion attempt at Wake Island. By December 12, Ro-60 and Ro-61 had set off from Kwajalein to aid a more robust Japanese invasion plan for Wake Island, with

Ro-62 joining two days later.

On December 21, while on the surface near Wake Island, a US Marine Corps F4F Wildcat from VMF-211 targeted Ro-60, strafing and dropping two bombs on her. While Ro-60 managed a crash dive, the assault damaged her periscopes and some diving tanks. Surfacing that night revealed the extent of the damages, which left her unfit for diving. After the fall of Wake Island to Japan on December 23, both Ro-60 and Ro-62 were ordered to head back to Kwajalein. However, on December 29, while nearing Kwajalein Atoll, Ro-60 ran aground on a reef, sustaining significant damages. Rescue and salvage operations, overseen by the Submarine Squadron 7 commander from the submarine tender Jingei, were undertaken, but the Ro-60's condition worsened. With the ship tilting dangerously, the crew discarded classified documents and abandoned her. Thankfully, Jingei rescued all 66 crew members.

Battle of Bataan

In 1936, Douglas MacArthur was designated as the Field Marshal of the Philippine army, tasked with crafting a formidable defense prior to its 1946 independence. U.S. Army Chief of Staff, General George C. Marshall, aimed to fortify the Philippines to the point where it could deter a Japanese invasion, hoping that the potential challenges in capturing the Philippines would dissuade Japan from entering the war. MacArthur believed he had until April 1942 to form a battle-ready force.

By 26 July 1941, MacArthur was reactivated in the US army, ascending to the rank of lieutenant general. In August, he activated one regiment from each of his ten reserve divisions, integrating them into the US military. On 27 November, he was alerted to the unpredictable nature of potential Japanese actions, with a strong possibility of aggression. The advisory noted that if a conflict was inevitable, Japan should be the one to initiate. By 18 December, a mere ten days post the commencement of hostilities, MacArthur activated the remaining reserve forces. The Philippine Army swelled to 120,000 troops, with 76,750 stationed on Luzon. However, as the Japanese Fourteenth Area Army, led by Masaharu Homma, advanced, and General Jonathan Wainwright's troops in North Luzon receded, MacArthur directed his Far East Air Force to relocate south to Bataan on 24 December. This move caused Lewis H. Brereton to leave major strategic locations, relocating to gravel airstrips in places like Pilar, Bataan. By the end of December, Bataan hosted 15,000 Americans, 65,000 Filipinos, and 26,000 refugees. While there was a decent accumulation of munitions by year's end, food stock was critically low, only covering about two months compared to the six months previously planned.

In a final combined effort by the Far East Air Force, U.S. aircraft managed to inflict damage on two Japanese transport ships, a destroyer, and sink a minesweeper. Nonetheless, these aerial and naval offensives barely hindered the Japanese advance.

When MacArthur was reinstated to active service, the most recent defense plan for the Philippine Islands, dubbed WPO-3, had been finalized in April 1941. This plan was an evolution of the joint Army-Navy War Plan Orange from 1938, anticipating conflict between the U.S. and Japan. WPO-3's strategy was twofold: firstly, to safeguard the entrance to Manila Bay, denying Japanese naval forces access, and secondly, to repel enemy land invasions. In case of overpowering enemy forces, a fallback to the Bataan Peninsula was advised. Bataan, pivotal for controlling Manila Bay, was to be staunchly defended. The defense would not only involve regular U.S. Army troops but also lean on the Philippine Army, which was shaped and trained under General MacArthur's guidance.

However, Navy assessments in April 1941 projected that the Pacific Fleet would need a minimum of two years to navigate across the Pacific and confront the enemy. Early 1941 Army projections were bleak too, forecasting that provisions would be depleted in six months, leading to the garrison's collapse. MacArthur, taking charge of the Allied army in July 1941, was critical of WPO-3, viewing it as pessimistic. He championed a bolder strategy that envisaged a defense encompassing the entire archipelago. His proposals were influential in the final plan's formulation. Following Washington's endorsement, War Plan Rainbow 5 was executed, emphasizing a defense strategy spanning the entire archipelago. Supplies essential for the defense were strategically placed behind beachfronts to support the defensive units against potential invasions. However, reverting to War Plan Orange 3 implied that the required supplies for a predicted six-month defense in Bataan were not sufficiently stocked for the retreating defenders.

When the Japanese initiated their landings on Luzon on the 10th and 12th of December, MacArthur did not confront them directly. He astutely deduced that these landings were meant to establish forward air bases and did not indicate a push towards Manila from these positions. Believing the situation wasn't alarming enough to modify his strategy, MacArthur chose to continue with his plan to robustly resist the primary Japanese assault at the shorelines. Thus, MacArthur's initial plan remained unaltered.

On the 20th of December, the submarine USS Stingray identified a massive convoy of troop vessels escorted by warships. This was General Homma's landing brigade comprising 85 transport vessels, two battleships, six cruisers, and roughly two dozen destroyers. Three submarines - the USS Stingray, USS Saury, and USS Salmon - took on the convoy, launching several torpedoes. However, due to faulty detonators in the Mark XIV torpedoes, most did not explode. Ultimately, only two transport ships were sunk before Japanese destroyers repelled the attacking submarines.

MacArthur planned to strategically relocate his troops, ensuring they were equipped and supplied, to their designated defensive points. Tasked with stalling the primary Japanese onslaught and maintaining the Bataan route accessible for Major General George Parker's South Luzon Force, Wainwright's North Luzon Force carried out their orders efficiently, despite the prevailing disorder.

On 22 December, Homma's principal unit of the 14th Area Army made its landing at Lingayen Gulf. The defending forces were unable to secure the shorelines, and by day's end, the Japanese had achieved most of their targets, setting themselves up to advance onto the central terrain. Four Filipino divisions—the 21st, 71st, 11th, and 91st—along with a Philippine Scouts battalion supported by a handful of tanks, were positioned against Homma's forces. The Japanese soon engaged with the Filipino 71st Division along Route 3, a road leading straight to Manila. While the American artillery initially halted the Japanese advancement, the combined force of Japanese aircraft and tanks eventually dispersed the Filipino infantry, leaving their artillery unprotected. On 23 December, another Japanese division landed south of Manila at Lamon Bay and commenced their northern progression.

Homma's 14th Area Army made its primary landing at Lingayen Gulf on 22 December's morning. The beach defenses were quickly overcome. By day's end, the Japanese had accomplished most of their goals, preparing to move into the central plains. Opposing Homma were four Filipino divisions: the 21st, 71st, 11th, and 91st, alongside a Philippine Scouts battalion supported by a few tanks. The Japanese soon encountered the Filipino 71st Division along Route 3, a main road leading to Manila. American artillery initially halted the Japanese, but their planes and tanks eventually overpowered the Filipino infantry, leaving their artillery exposed. On 23 December, another Japanese division landed at Lamon Bay, to the south of Manila, and progressed northwards.

Recognizing the unstoppable Japanese advance, Wainwright communicated with MacArthur's Manila headquarters on the evening of 23 December, stating that defending Lingayen beaches further was unfeasible. He sought and was granted permission to retreat behind the Agno River. MacArthur faced a decision: either stand strong at the Agno River, bolstering Wainwright with his top unit, the Philippine Division, or strategically fall back to Bataan. He chose the latter, altering his original defensive strategy and reverting to a previous plan. By the night of 23 December, MacArthur informed all commanders that they were now following "WPO-3."

In the midst of this, on 24 December, President Manuel L. Quezon of the Philippine Commonwealth, along with his family and officials, were relocated to Corregidor. This included the USAFFE headquarters. Additionally, MacArthur had all USAFFE military staff evacuated from main urban zones. By 26 December, Manila was officially designated an open city. This decision was broadcasted and printed, but the Japanese learned of it via the radio. Subsequently, they bombed the port, targeting supplies destined for Bataan and Corregidor.

In the initial days of January 1942, the 11th Division under Brigadier General William E. Brougher and the 21st Division led by Brigadier General Mateo Capinpin, aided by the 26th Cavalry Regiment, engaged in a strategic retreat along the Guagua-Porac Line. From the afternoon of 2 January, the Japanese 9th Infantry pushed the 21st Division from Porac, relocating them to defensive positions south of the Gumain River by 4 January. Concurrently, from 3 January, the Japanese 2nd Formosa Infantry drove the 11th Infantry from Guagua to Lubao, and eventually to the Gumain River by 5 January. On the subsequent days of 5 and 6 January, both the 21st and 11th Divisions retreated across the Culo River, entering Bataan.

Brigadier General Clyde A. Selleck was tasked with setting up and maintaining a defensive stance at Layac. The intention was for him to hold this position for a few days to allow for the Abucay Line's preparation. For this duty, Selleck had the American 31st Infantry, Scout 26th Cavalry, and the Philippine 71st and 72nd infantry regiments from the 71st Division at his disposal. These troops took their positions on 3 January. By 6 January, they faced an assault from the Imai Detachment, led by Hifumi Imai. As the day progressed and more Japanese forces approached, Parker granted Selleck the approval to retreat during the night.

The Bataan peninsula was spanned by two distinct defensive lines: the Mauban line stretching 8,000 yards on the west, manned by the I Philippine Corps, and the longer Abucay line spanning 15,000 yards on the east, held by the II Philippine Corps. Wainwright oversaw the I Philippine Corps, composed of 22,500 personnel. This included the units led by General Fidel Segundo, Brigadier Generals Clifford Bluemel, and Luther R. Stevens, as well as the 26th Cavalry. Meanwhile, Parker was in charge of the II Philippine Corps with 25,000 soldiers, which encompassed the 11th, 21st, divisions led by Brigadier Generals Vicente Lim and Albert M. Jones, and the 57th Infantry. The 515th Coast Artillery and the 200th Infantry Regiment provided anti aircraft cover, while the 192nd and 194th Tank Battalions gave armored support. Two mountains, Mount Natib and Mount Silanganan, geographically separated the two corps. Their rugged landscapes were deemed untraversable, creating a lack of direct communication between the corps, resulting in a significant vulnerability.

Confronting the Allies was Akira Nara's 65th Brigade, which was initially designated for mere garrison roles, especially since the 48th Division had been sent to Java. Consequently, the Japanese had a strength of 23,222 soldiers on Bataan, opposed by 15,000 Americans and 65,000 Filipinos. On 10 January, MacArthur made a morale-boosting tour amongst his Bataan forces, journeying from Limay to Abucay. Nara's strategy for assailing the II Corps involved deploying the 141st Infantry against the 57th Infantry on his eastern side and using the 9th Infantry on his west, aiming to overrun the II Corps' left wing. He kept the 142nd Infantry in reserve.

On 9 January, Nara launched his assault, mainly targeting the 57th Infantry. By 11 January, they had reached the primary defensive line, and the next day, Parker dispatched his reserve 21st Infantry to reinforce the 57th. On the same day, the 52nd Infantry under Brigadier General Virgilio N. Cordero Jr., known as "Bicol's Own", was positioned to fill a breach on the 51st Division's right flank. By 14 January, in an effort to strengthen the 41st Division, Bluemel's 31st Division was transferred from I Corps, led by Wainwright, to II Corps under Parker. Observing the increasing gap between the two Corps, Richard J. Marshall, MacArthur's Deputy Chief of Staff positioned at Mt. Mariveles' Signal Hill, dispatched Brigadier General Maxon S. Lough's Philippine Division, which comprised the Scout 45th Infantry and the American 31st Infantry, to the frontlines.

During intense combat on 12 January, 2nd Lieutenant Alexander R. Nininger, a platoon leader from the 57th Infantry, displayed exceptional bravery. With only a rifle and grenades, he confronted the enemy in direct combat, enabling his team to regain control of Abucay Hacienda. Nininger posthumously received the Medal of Honor. Another commendable act came from Filipino soldier Narciso Ortilano. When ambushed by a Japanese unit, he fiercely defended his position, eliminating many adversaries even after his machine gun malfunctioned. He was honored with the Distinguished Service Cross for his valor.

The following day, Jones' 51st Division, on Parker's orders, launched a counteroffensive. They faced fierce resistance from the Japanese 141st Infantry and the 9th Infantry on their left. Despite creating an opening in the Abucay Line, the Japanese didn't capitalize on it. The 141st redirected its attack towards the 41st Division, while the 9th shifted their focus to Mount Natib. John R. Boatwright's 53rd Infantry, positioned on the 51st Division's left, was instructed to pull back and reestablish contact with I Corps. By day's end, the 51st Division was incapacitated, but the 41st Division under Lim remained steadfast. By 18 January, the Japanese halted their onslaught, and Nara's artillery and 7th Tank Regiment were withdrawn.

MacArthur, on 17 January, communicated to Washington about the deteriorating food situation. The same day saw the 31st Infantry being directed to reestablish the main defense line, with subsequent relief by the 11th Division. The 45th Infantry joined the offensive on 18 January, but both units struggled against intensified Japanese assaults. Both sides suffered heavy losses. By 22 January, the Philippine Division had been pushed back to their original positions from 19 January. Moreover, the Japanese 9th Infantry managed to navigate the side of Mount Natib, entering Guitol, situated behind the II Corps defenses.

On 10 January, the Japanese took control of Olongapo and Grande Island. By 15 January, Homa handed over the charge of western Bataan to Naoki Kimura's Detachment. This consisted of the 122nd Infantry positioned on the West Road and the 20th Infantry situated on the inland flank near Mount Silanganan. After the 31st Division was transferred to II Corps, Wainwright led the 1st Division, 91st Division, and the 26th Cavalrymen. The Japanese forces launched an assault on Moron on 16 January. This prompted Wainwright to position his 72nd Infantry along the Pilar-Bagac Road, just behind his primary defensive line. By 20 January, while the Japanese 122nd Infantry engaged the 1st Division, the 20th Infantry managed to breach Wainwright's eastern defenses, establishing a roadblock on the West Road by the following day. Due to this blockade, northern troops faced difficulties in accessing essential supplies like food and ammunition.

On 22 January, citing a significant breach at the heart of the primary battle-front, MacArthur commanded a strategic pullback to the Pilar-Bagac Road. By 25 January, the I Corps initiated its retreat. Those located north of the roadblock, under the leadership of Kearie Berry, attempted to navigate the coastline towards Bagac. However, they were compelled to leave behind their trucks and artillery.

Engagements took place at Longoskawayan Point between January 22 to February 1, at Quinauan Point from January 22 to February 8, and at Silalim-Anyasan between January 27 to February 13. These confrontations were grouped under the umbrella term, "Battle of the Points". The outcome was the complete annihilation of the Japanese 1st and 2nd Battalions, 20th Infantry.

On the evening of January 22, in an effort to sidestep the I Corps and isolate the service command area led by USAFFE deputy commander Brigadier General Allan C. McBride, 900 Japanese soldiers from the 2nd Battalion, 20th Infantry, 16th Division, commanded by Nariyoshi Tsunehiro, made a landing on southern Bataan's western shore. Although their intended landing point was Caibobo Point, they were intercepted by PT-34, causing two of their barges to sink. Subsequently, 300 of these troops landed at Longoskawayan Point and the remaining 600 at Quinauan Point. Philippine Constabulary regiments, Francis J. Bridget's Naval Battalion, Battery Geary's gunfire, support from USS Quail, tanks from the 192nd Tank Battalion, and personnel from the 34th and 21st Pursuit Squadrons effectively countered the Japanese forces. Prominent figures in this engagement included Clinton A. Pierce, Mariano Castañeda,

Pelagio Cruz, Ed Dyess, and Ray C. Hunt. Eventually, with support from the 57th and 45th Infantry units, the Japanese advance was rolled back.

The naval infantry comprised 150 ground crew from Patrol Wing Ten, 80 sailors from the Cavite Naval Ammunition Depot, and 130 sailors from USS Canopus, bolstered by 120 sailors from facilities at Cavite, Olongapo, and Mariveles, and 120 Marines from an anti-aircraft unit. Machine guns salvaged from damaged aircraft of Patrol Wing Ten were repurposed in the Canopus machine shop. While the Marines were integrated into the ranks, sailors were guided by the Marine's expertise. Trying to adapt their white uniforms for jungle combat, sailors dyed them with coffee, resulting in a peculiar yellow hue. A found diary of a Japanese officer referred to them as a boisterous suicide squad with strikingly vivid uniforms, attempting to bait enemy fire to expose their positions.

On January 25, Homma directed the 16th Division commander, Susumu Morioka, to deploy 200 soldiers to reinforce the Quinauan Point beachhead. However, another misdirected landing occurred on January 27, causing the troops to disembark between the Anyasan and Silaiim rivers. The 17th Pursuit Squadron and 2nd Constabulary contained them. By January 29, the 45th Infantry sent additional troops. On February 1, Mitsuo Kimura's 1st Battalion, 20th Infantry, was directed towards Quinauan Point with orders to capture Mount Mariveles. The subsequent day, his battalion, aided by the Yaeyama, faced aerial and land-based attacks while on their barges. The remnants retreated to Silaiim Point. Command of the defensive line was taken over by Edmund J. Lilly and Harold Keith Johnson, incorporating elements of the 12th and 57th Infantry, alongside tanks from the 192nd Tank Battalion. Subsequent Japanese efforts to flee by sea starting from February 7 were thwarted. Lastly, a frantic attempt by 200 Japanese troops to advance northwards from the point was unsuccessful.

On January 26, the 65th Brigade under Nara's command was tasked to chase the withdrawing Filipino and American troops. Nara anticipated the upcoming defensive barrier would stretch from Limay to Mount Mariveles. With this assumption, he moved to confront the Orion-Bagac line, believing it to be a mere outer defense. His plan was to push south via Trail 2, then follow the eastern base of Mount Samat. Facing him were forces led by Bluemel. On January 27, Nara initiated his assault using the 9th and 141st infantry against the 51st Infantry positioned south of the Pilar River. The 41st Infantry joined to back the 51st on January 28. The battle raged on until January 29, when Nara received orders to reassign the 9th Infantry to the 16th Division. Seeing an opportunity, Bluemel chose to strike back on February 2, deploying the 41st Infantry, 51st Combat Team, and the 31st Engineer Battalion. They were flanked on the left by the 21st Division and on the right by the 32nd Infantry. By February 8, it became clear that the 65th Brigade's offensives had been unsuccessful, resulting in heavy casualties. Consequently, Nara received directions to retreat northwards towards the Pilar-Bagac Road.

On January 28, under the leadership of Hiroshi Nakanishi and Yorimasa Yoshioka, the 3rd Battalion and the 20th Infantry staff mounted an attack on I Corps' Orion-Bagac line. They successfully infiltrated the rear of the 1st Division along the Tuol River. The Japanese forces were split into two groups: a smaller contingent referred to as the "Little Pocket" and a larger group of around 1000 men dubbed the "Big Pocket". By February 5, Wainwright had deployed an impressive force, including five companies from the 1st Division, two battalions from the 92nd Infantry, a Scout battalion, a Constabulary battalion, tanks from the 192nd Tank Battalion, and artillery from the 24th Field Artillery, all to counter the Japanese advancement and eradicate the two pockets. The situation evolved on February 6 when a salient, named the "Upper Pocket", was formed by the Japanese 122nd Infantry and 2nd Battalion, 33rd Infantry, drawing within 800 yards of the Big Pocket. By February 7, the 1st Division had encircled the Little Pocket, which was eradicated by February 9. With the Little Pocket dealt with, focus shifted to the Big Pocket, and by February 10, Trail 7 was under control. Yoshioka, on February 11, endeavored to move northward in sync with the 14th Army's broader retreat across Bataan. By February 15, 377 of the Japanese had successfully returned to their own positions, and the Upper Pocket was left behind. By February 26, following the defeat of the Japanese 20th Infantry, the I Corps' defensive line was reinstated.

On February 3, 1st Lieutenant Willibald C. Bianchi from the 45th Infantry, Philippine Scouts, spearheaded a platoon against two opposing machine-gun positions. Using grenades, he neutralized them. Despite suffering two bullet wounds to his chest, he operated an antiaircraft machine gun until a third serious injury forced him off his position.

By February 8, General Homma realized his effective forces on Bataan were reduced to three infantry battalions. He commanded a halt and his army retreated, taking positions further from the front, awaiting reinforcements. Homma's team felt a strong spiritual influence from the enduring American resistance on Bataan. This resistance symbolized American loyalty to the Filipinos, reassuring them of continuous support. Meanwhile, MacArthur's Bataan army was isolated and barely surviving on meager supplies.

On February 20, notable Filipino officials, including President Manuel L. Quezon, Vice President Sergio Osmeña, Chief Justice José Abad Santos, were safely evacuated via the Swordfish. Two days later, MacArthur received orders to depart. General Wainwright took command of all forces in the Philippines, while General Edward P. King assumed control of Luzon. Command structures shifted, with Jones leading I Corps, Parker overseeing II Corps, and Lewis C. Beebe appointed as MacArthur's deputy chief of staff.

On March 12, MacArthur, along with his family and staff, departed from Corregidor to Mindanao, using four PT boats led by Lieutenant Commander John D. Bulkeley. Recognized for his valor and service over several months, Bulkeley was awarded multiple commendations, including the Medal of Honor. MacArthur, upon reaching Australia, made his iconic pledge, "I Shall Return."

Washington updated Wainwright about MacArthur's safety on March 17. They also discussed supply strategies, which involved blockade runners and submarines. However, many of these operations faced difficulties, and by February's end, essential supplies like rice and flour were exhausted.

Changes in Japanese leadership occurred on February 23, with Homma's chief of staff, Masami Maeda, replaced by Takaji Wachi. Wachi and his team prepared for an April assault, bolstering their forces with reinforcements. Wachi noted the formidable resistance by the Philippine Army, especially their artillery firepower. Hence, they augmented their artillery resources and also strengthened their air brigade. On March 22, an honorable surrender proposal from the Japanese, citing other nations' defeats, was dismissed by King.

As of April 3, King's Luzon Force was comprised of 79,000 troops, but they were debilitated by malnutrition, diseases, and exhaustion. The force had a limited air capability with only two P40s and two P-35s remaining. The divisions were strategically placed, with varying divisions guarding different sectors of I Corps and II Corps.

On April 3rd, at 3:00 PM, Homma initiated his assault on the Orion Bagac Line. He hoped to break through the II Corps defense by exploiting its left flank at Mount Samat, ultimately heading southeast towards Manila Bay. Concurrently, on March 23, the Japanese began aerial raids.

At 9:00 AM on April 3rd, Kitajima's massive 196-gun assault began, followed by 150 flights from Mikamai's 22nd Air Brigade. By 3:00 PM, Nara's troops were advancing through the trails between the Catamon and Pantingan Rivers, and Kitano's division was also making progress. By day's end, Lim's troops were on the back foot.

The 4th of April saw a continuation of Japanese artillery and air raids. Nara's forces kept moving southwards as the 41st Division retreated. The onslaught from the Japanese left and right wings forced a further retreat of the 21st Division. To stave off a complete breakdown of Sector D, King dispatched the

Luzon Force reserves.

By April 5th, the Japanese forces seized Mt. Samat. Sector C's 51st Combat Team found themselves under attack. In a bid to bolster defenses, Wainwright ordered a counterattack. Yet, the weakened state of the troops rendered this move ineffective. Their defenses crumbled, forcing them to the San Vicente River's east bank. Homma's strategies over six days had devastated significant portions of the defending army.

On April 7th, the Japanese continued their offensive. Bluemel's defenses gave way, leading to further retreats. Homma's forces had achieved in less than a week what was anticipated to take a month, and with negligible losses.

By April 8th, Bluemel's troops were in further retreat. An indication of an impending surrender came with the message about a car with a white flag. King believed further resistance was futile, and Wainwright informed MacArthur of the dire situation. Vital assets were destroyed or evacuated as the last of the aerial fleet left Bataan.

The defenders were in disarray as I Corps and the shattered remains of II Corps retreated. Commanders struggled to maintain communication, relying on sporadic contact by foot messenger. A mass exodus of troops and refugees clogged the roads.

On April 9th, King's negotiations with the Japanese began. However, the discussions hit a snag as the Japanese demanded the surrender of all Philippine forces. Following further discussions, no formal surrender document was executed or signed, leaving the surrender somewhat ambiguous.

The persistent defense of Bataan, even after key regions like Singapore and the Indies were conquered, was a beacon of hope for the Allies. However, the prolonged defense can largely be attributed to the strategic reassignment of the 48th Division from Homma's troops during a pivotal phase and the depletion of his remaining force. Notably, the Japanese army had a more strenuous task conquering Malaya and Singapore than Homma did with Bataan and Corregidor.

Bataan's surrender precipitated Corregidor's fall a month later. Some posit that without this resistance, the rapid Japanese advance could have swiftly engulfed all U.S. bases in the Pacific and even led to the invasion of Australia. MacArthur's intelligence officer, Willoughby, postulated post-war that the significant resistance in Bataan and Corregidor substantially hampered the Japanese wartime schedule, inhibiting them from committing sufficient resources to secure Guadalcanal. Conversely, Gavin Long believed that the Japanese deliberately extended Luzon's resistance to expedite their conquest of the Indies.

Historian Teodoro Agoncillo opined that the battle was futile, as it need-lessly cost lives without serving a strategic objective. According to him, only Yamashita considered invading Australia, a plan not backed by Tojo. Homma even believed that the USAFFE could have retaken Manila given their numerical advantage.

The Japanese's overarching war strategy faced significant delays due to the resistance at Bataan and Corregidor. The Imperial General Headquarters was frustrated by the protracted battles since they had initially hoped for a swift victory in the Philippines by mid-February. After the Allies' final surrender in the Philippines in June 1942, Homma was dismissed and relegated to a desk job for the war's remainder.

Tragically, over 75,000 Filipino and American POWs were subjected to the infamous Bataan Death March. Yet, approximately 10,000-12,000 escaped, forming guerrilla groups that challenged the Japanese occupiers. In a tragic event, the Japanese ship Shinyō Maru, carrying U.S. POWs, was sunk by the USS Paddle, leading to the death of 668 POWs, with 82 survivors.

Years later, MacArthur spearheaded the Philippines' liberation campaign, fulfilling his promise to return. This initiative included the Battle for Bataan's recapture, symbolically avenging the initial surrender to the Japanese invaders.

Battle of the Coral Sea

O n 8 December 1941, which was 7 December in U.S. time, Japan launched attacks on the British territories of Malaya, Singapore, and Hong Kong, as well as the U.S. naval base at Pearl Harbor, subsequently declaring war on both the U.S. and the British Empire. The Japanese leadership initiated these hostilities with the aim of incapacitating the U.S. naval presence, securing territories abundant in natural resources, and acquiring strategic military bases to fortify their expansive empire. As outlined in the Imperial Japanese Navy Combined Fleet's "Secret Order Number One" from 1 November 1941, the primary objectives for Japan's early wartime campaigns were to drive out British and American forces from the Netherlands Indies and the Philippines and to pursue a policy of self-reliance and economic independence.

In alignment with these objectives, during the early months of 1942, Japanese forces expanded their reach, capturing the Philippines, Singapore, the Dutch East Indies, Wake Island, New Britain, the Gilbert Islands, and Guam. They dealt significant damage to the Allied forces on land, sea, and air. The intention was to use these newly acquired territories to form a defensive ring around their empire, from which they could fend off and wear down any counterattacks from the Allies.

At the war's onset, Japan's Naval General Staff contemplated invading Northern Australia to curb its potential as a base that could jeopardize Japan's southern defensive perimeter. However, the Imperial Japanese Army dismissed this, citing a lack of necessary resources and capacity for such an operation. Meanwhile, Vice Admiral Shigeyoshi Inoue, who led the IJN's Fourth Fleet (also known as the South Seas Force) and oversaw the majority of naval units in the South Pacific, championed occupying Tulagi in the Solomon Islands and Port Moresby in New Guinea. Capturing these would bring Northern Australia within the reach of Japanese land-based planes. Furthermore, Inoue perceived that taking control of these areas would bolster the defense of the pivotal Japanese base at Rabaul, located on New Britain. The military's higher echelons concurred with Inoue, proposing extended campaigns leveraging these new assets to target New Caledonia, Fiji, and Samoa, thus disrupting Australia's communication and supply channels with the U.S.

By April 1942, the Japanese military had formulated Operation Mo, aiming to seize Port Moresby by 10 May through a maritime assault and capture Tulagi between 2-3 May. This strategy intended for Tulagi to host a seaplane facility that could facilitate air raids against Allied positions in the South Pacific and serve as a reconnaissance base. Once Mo was executed, the Japanese navy anticipated initiating Operation RY to take over Nauru and Ocean Island by 15 May, coveted for their phosphate resources. Subsequent campaigns against Fiji, Samoa, and New Caledonia (dubbed Operation FS) would be devised post the completion of Mo and RY. However, after a detrimental airstrike by the Allies on Japanese naval forces near Lae-Salamaua in New Guinea in March, Inoue sought air protection from the Combined Fleet for Mo. He expressed particular concerns about Allied aircraft in Townsville and Cooktown, Australia, which were out of reach for his Rabaul and Lae-based bombers.

In parallel, Admiral Isoroku Yamamoto, at the helm of the Combined Fleet, strategized an operation slated for June, aiming to bait the untouched U.S. Navy's carriers (post-Pearl Harbor) into a decisive face-off near Midway Atoll. While focusing on this, Yamamoto allocated several of his powerful vessels, inclusive of two main carriers, a light carrier, a group of cruisers, and two destroyer contingents, to back Operation Mo, delegating the naval aspect of this mission to Inoue.

The U.S. Navy, spearheaded by the Communication Security Section of the Office of Naval Communications, had been making significant headway in decoding Japanese communication protocols for years. By March 1942, they were able to decipher roughly 15% of the IJN's Ro or Naval Codebook D code, referred to as "JN-25B" by the U.S., which the IJN utilized for approximately half of its messages. By April's end, the U.S. was decoding nearly 85% of the messages encoded in the Ro code.

In March 1942, U.S. intelligence identified mentions of the MO operation in intercepted communications. An intercepted IJN message on 5 April directed a carrier and other sizable vessels towards Inoue's operational region. On 13 April, the British decoded an IJN message revealing the movement of the Fifth Carrier Division, inclusive of the Shōkaku and Zuikaku fleet carriers, towards Inoue's command, starting from Formosa via the central IJN base at Truk. The British relayed this information to the U.S., theorizing that Port Moresby might be the focal point of MO.

U.S. Admiral Chester W. Nimitz and his team, after reviewing the decoded messages, surmised that a significant Japanese campaign targeting Port Moresby was imminent by early May. The Allies considered Port Moresby crucial for a counteroffensive, led by General Douglas MacArthur, against Japanese units in the Southwest Pacific. Additionally, Nimitz's team predicted potential Japanese carrier strikes on Samoa and Suva. Nimitz, in coordination with Admiral Ernest King, resolved to counteract the Japanese plan by mobilizing all four available Pacific Fleet carriers towards the Coral Sea. By 27 April, further intelligence solidified the specifics of the MO and RY strategies.

On 29 April, Nimitz dispatched his four carriers and associated vessels to the Coral Sea. Task Force 17, spearheaded by Rear Admiral Fletcher and comprising the carrier Yorktown alongside other supporting ships, was already operating in the South Pacific. TF 11, led by Rear Admiral Aubrey Fitch, featured the carrier Lexington and was positioned between Fiji and New Caledonia. TF 16, under Vice Admiral William F. Halsey, had just returned from the Doolittle Raid in the central Pacific to Pearl Harbor and immediately set out again. However, TF 16 would be late for the impending conflict. Nimitz delegated command to Fletcher until Halsey arrived with TF 16. Although the Coral Sea jurisdiction fell under MacArthur, both Fletcher and Halsey were instructed to liaise directly with Nimitz.

The Japanese, interpreting non-coded radio chatter from TF 16, mistakenly believed that the majority of the U.S. Navy carriers were in the central Pacific. The whereabouts of the remaining carrier were unknown to them, leading them to underestimate potential U.S. carrier interventions in the MO operation until it was significantly underway.

In the latter part of April, Japanese submarines Ro-33 and Ro-34 scouted the regions where they intended to make landings. Their exploration covered Rossel Island, the Deboyne Group anchorage within the Louisiade Archipelago, Jomard Channel, and the pathway leading to Port Moresby from the east. They did not encounter any Allied vessels in their survey and made their way back to Rabaul on the 23rd and 24th of April.

The force set to invade Port Moresby, overseen by Rear Admiral Kōsō Abe, consisted of 11 transport vessels bearing roughly 5,000 soldiers from the IJA's South Seas Detachment and an additional 500 personnel from the 3rd Kure Special Naval Landing Force. The Port Moresby Attack Force, which included one light cruiser and six aging Kamikaze and Mutsuki-class destroyers led by Rear Admiral Sadamichi Kajioka, was tasked with guarding the transports. Abe's fleet left Rabaul on 4 May for the 840 nautical mile journey to Port Moresby, merging with Kajioka's group the following day. Navigating at a speed of 8 knots, they intended to use the Jomard Channel in the Louisiades as a passageway around New Guinea's southern end, targeting a 10 May arrival at Port Moresby. The Allied defense at Port Moresby had a strength of approximately 5,333 personnel. However, only half were infantry and they were inadequately equipped and poorly trained.

Spearheading the assault on Tulagi was the Tulagi Assault Group under Rear Admiral Kiyohide Shima. This group comprised two minelayers, two vintage Mutsuki-class destroyers, five minesweepers, two subchasers, and a transport ship carrying roughly 400 soldiers from the 3rd Kure SNLF. Providing backup for this force was the Covering Group, led by Rear Admiral Aritomo Gotō, which included the light carrier Shōhō, four Furutaka/Aoba-class heavy cruisers, and a destroyer. An auxiliary Cover Force, under Rear Admiral Kuninori Marumo, was equipped with two light cruisers, a seaplane tender, and three gunboats. After Tulagi's capture on 3 or 4 May, both the Covering Group and the Cover Force were set to shift positions to protect the Port Moresby invasion. Overseeing the MO operation aboard the cruiser Kashima, Inoue reached Rabaul from Truk on 4 May.

On 28 April, Gotō's contingent departed from Truk, navigating the Solomons between Bougainville and Choiseul, and established their position near New Georgia Island. Marumo's team left New Ireland on 29 April, aiming for Thousand Ships Bay on Santa Isabel Island to set up a seaplane base on 2 May in support of the Tulagi attack. Shima's troops left Rabaul on 30 April.

The Carrier Attack Group, which included the carriers Zuikaku and Shōkaku, two heavy cruisers, and six destroyers, departed from Truk on 1 May. Led by Vice Admiral Takeo Takagi and having Rear Admiral Chūichi Hara in charge of the carrier air wings, their objective was to descend the eastern Solomon Islands and access the Coral Sea below Guadalcanal. Their mission was to offer air protection for invasion troops, neutralize Allied air forces in Port Moresby, and confront and obliterate any Allied naval units entering the Coral Sea.

While heading to the Coral Sea, Takagi's carriers were tasked with delivering nine Zero fighter jets to Rabaul. However, inclement weather on 2-3 May forced a return of the aircraft to the carriers. Due to this setback, and to stick to the MO schedule, Takagi decided to forgo another delivery attempt and redirected his group to the Solomon Islands for refueling.

For early alerts of incoming Allied naval forces, Japanese submarines I-22, I-24, I-28, and I-29 were positioned in a line roughly 450 nautical miles southwest of Guadalcanal. Fletcher's troops, however, had already reached the Coral Sea before these submarines were in place, keeping them hidden from the Japanese. Another submarine, I-21, dispatched to scout around Nouméa, was targeted by aircraft from the Yorktown on 2 May but evaded damage. Meanwhile, submarines Ro-33 and Ro-34 were positioned to encircle Port Moresby, arriving on 5 May, but didn't engage in any battles.

On 1 May's early hours, TF 17 and TF 11 converged approximately 350 mi to the northwest of New Caledonia. Immediately upon joining forces, Fletcher dispatched TF 11 to replenish their fuel supply from the tanker Tippecanoe, while TF 17 drew fuel from Neosho. By the following day, TF 17 had completed its refueling operations. However, TF 11 indicated that their refueling would extend until 4 May. In response, Fletcher decided to move TF 17 northwest in the direction of the Louisiades. He directed TF 11 to rendezvous with TF 44, which was traveling from Sydney and Nouméa, once their fueling was done on 4 May. Commanded by Australian Rear Admiral John Crace under MacArthur's jurisdiction, TF 44 was a combined Australia-U.S. naval unit comprising cruisers HMAS Australia, Hobart, USS Chicago, and three accompanying destroyers. After fueling TF 11, Tippecanoe left the Coral Sea, heading to Efate to supply other Allied vessels with its remaining fuel.

In the dawn hours of 3 May, Shima's unit approached Tulagi and began the process of deploying naval infantry to secure the island. Surprisingly, Tulagi was unguarded. A small unit consisting of Australian commandos and a Royal Australian Air Force reconnaissance squad had vacated the island just prior to Shima's arrival. Immediately after landing, the Japanese began to establish a seaplane and communication base. Planes from Shōhō provided cover for the landing operations until the afternoon, after which Gotō's fleet made its way to Bougainville for refueling, anticipating the upcoming Port Moresby landings.

At 5 pm on 3 May, Fletcher received intelligence that the Japanese invasion force was spotted approaching the southern Solomons the previous day. Fletcher was unaware that TF 11 had managed to refuel ahead of time that morning and was a mere 69 mi east of TF 17. However, due to Fletcher's directive to keep radio communications silent, TF 11 couldn't relay this information. Redirecting its path, TF 17 sped at 31 mph towards Guadalcanal, preparing to launch aerial assaults on the Japanese contingent at Tulagi the next day.

On the morning of 4 May, from a location about 120 mi south of Guadalcanal, TF 17 deployed a series of three air raids against Shima's units using a combined force of 60 aircraft. The aircraft from Yorktown caught Shima's fleet off-guard, sinking the destroyer Kikuzuki and three minesweepers, inflicting damage on several other vessels, and eliminating four seaplanes assisting the landings. The U.S. incurred losses, including one torpedo aircraft and two fighter planes, but all crew members were eventually saved. After retrieving its aircraft on the night of 4 May, TF 17 regrouped and moved southward. Despite the setbacks from the airstrikes, the Japanese remained committed to the seaplane base's establishment and commenced reconnaissance flights from Tulagi by 6 May.

Meanwhile, on 4 May, Takagi's Carrier Strike Force, which was refueling north of Tulagi, learned about Fletcher's airstrike. Takagi promptly halted refueling operations, steered southeast, and dispatched scout planes to scan the region east of the Solomons, assuming the presence of U.S. carriers. With no Allied vessels in that vicinity, the scouts came back empty-handed.

At dawn on 5 May, TF 17 joined forces with TF 11 and TF 44, meeting at a pre-set location 370 mi to the south of Guadalcanal. Simultaneously, four F4F Wildcat fighters from Yorktown engaged and downed a Kawanishi H6K reconnaissance plane from the Yokohama Air Group, stationed at the Shortland Islands, approximately 13 mi away from TF 11. Although the plane couldn't relay its findings before crashing, its absence led the Japanese to correctly speculate that it had been targeted by carrier-based aircraft.

Later, Fletcher received intelligence from Pearl Harbor, indicating that the Japanese intended to launch a troop landing operation at Port Moresby on 10 May, with their major aircraft carriers likely positioned near the invasion convoy. Armed with this crucial insight, Fletcher ordered TF 17 to undergo refueling from Neosho. Once refueling wrapped up on 6 May, Fletcher intended to navigate his units northwards, towards the Louisiades, preparing for a confrontation set for 7 May.

Meanwhile, on 5 May, Takagi's carrier group navigated along the eastern edge of the Solomons. They veered west, passing south of San Cristobal (Makira), and entered the Coral Sea, moving between Guadalcanal and Rennell Island during the early hours of 6 May. Positioned 210 mi west of Tulagi, Takagi began refueling, anticipating a carrier clash on the following day.

On 6 May, Fletcher merged TF 11 and TF 44 into TF 17. Under the impression that the Japanese carriers were still positioned far to the north, near Bougainville, he proceeded with refueling. The day's reconnaissance efforts from the U.S. carriers didn't spot any Japanese naval units, as they were just beyond the range of detection.

At 10:00, a Kawanishi scout plane from Tulagi detected TF 17 and relayed the information back. By 10:50, Takagi, who was around 350 mi to the north of Fletcher, received the intel. Considering this distance, launching an immediate attack wasn't feasible. Receiving word that Fletcher seemed to be increasing the gap, and given the overcast conditions that would make targeting challenging, Takagi dispatched his two carriers along with two destroyers under Hara's leadership. Moving at 23 mph, they aimed to be in striking range by dawn the next day. Meanwhile, Takagi continued refueling his remaining fleet.

On the same day, U.S. B-17 bombers from Australia, rerouted through Port Moresby, made several unsuccessful attempts to target the oncoming Port Moresby invasion troops, including Gotō's fleet. MacArthur's team informed Fletcher of these assaults and the positions of the Japanese invasion fleet. Reports from MacArthur's pilots of sighting a carrier, presumed to be Shōhō, located approximately 489 mi northwest of TF 17, further solidified Fletcher's belief that significant carriers were accompanying the invasion convoy.

By 18:00, TF 17 had finished refueling, and Fletcher directed Neosho, along with the destroyer Sims, to move further south to a predetermined meeting point. Subsequently, TF 17 shifted direction, heading northwest toward Rossel Island in the Louisiades. Unknown to both parties, by 20:00 that evening, their carriers were a mere 70 mi apart. At 20:00, Hara pivoted back to rendezvous with Takagi, who, having wrapped up refueling, was now moving toward Hara.

Either late on the 6th of May or in the early hours of the 7th, Kamikawa Maru established a seaplane base within the Deboyne Islands. This move was designed to bolster air support for the invasion units as they neared Port Moresby. Meanwhile, Marumo's Cover Force positioned themselves near the D'Entrecasteaux Islands, setting up a protective barrier for Abe's advancing convoy.

On 7 May, at 06:25, TF 17 found itself 132 mi south of Rossel Island. Fletcher then dispatched Crace's cruiser group, newly labeled Task Group 17.3, to secure the Jomard Passage. Fletcher was aware that by doing this, Crace would be operating without aerial support, since the carriers of TF 17 were focused on finding and targeting the Japanese carriers. Even though detaching Crace meant reducing the anti-aircraft defenses for his carriers, Fletcher believed this move was crucial to prevent the Japanese invasion forces from advancing to Port Moresby while he was occupied with the carriers.

Fletcher presumed that Takagi's carrier group was north of his location, around the Louisiades. Starting at 06:19, he ordered Yorktown to deploy 10 Douglas SBD Dauntless dive bombers to scout the area. On the other hand, Hara assumed that Fletcher's force was to his south and suggested Takagi dispatch aircraft to scan that region. Positioned about 350 mi east of Fletcher, Takagi launched 12 Nakajima B5Ns at 06:00 to look for TF 17. Simultaneously, Gotō's cruisers, Kinugasa and Furutaka, sent out four Kawanishi E7K2 Type 94 floatplanes to survey southeast of the Louisiades. Enhancing this search effort were several floatplanes from Deboyne, four Kawanishi H6Ks from Tulagi, and three Mitsubishi G4M bombers from Rabaul. Both sides had their carrier attack aircraft on standby, poised to spring into action once the enemy was pinpointed.

At 07:22, a scout plane from Takagi's carrier, Shōkaku, detected U.S. vessels at 182° (slightly west of due south), 188 mi from Takagi's position. By 07:45, the scout confirmed spotting "one carrier, one cruiser, and three destroyers." This sighting was quickly corroborated by another aircraft from Shōkaku. However, the aircraft had mistakenly identified the oiler Neosho and the destroyer Sims, previously dispatched southwards. Assuming he'd found the U.S. carriers, Hara, with Takagi's agreement, promptly sent out his entire available air fleet. By 08:15, 78 aircraft, comprising 18 Zero fighters, 36 Aichi D3A dive bombers, and 24 torpedo planes, launched from Shōkaku and Zuikaku and headed towards the reported location. Lieutenant Commander Kakuichi Takahashi took overall charge, while the torpedo bombers were led by Lieutenant Commander Shigekazu Shimazaki.

At 08:20, a plane from Furutaka located Fletcher's carriers, reporting back to Inoue's base at Rabaul. This information was relayed to Takagi. By 08:30, a floatplane from Kinugasa verified this sighting. Given the varying reports, Takagi and Hara chose to press on with their southern strike, while steering their carriers northwest to approach Furutaka's reported sighting. They speculated that the U.S. might be operating two distinct carrier groups.

At 08:15, John L. Nielsen, piloting a Yorktown SBD, spotted Gotō's group guarding the invasion convoy. Regrettably, Nielsen's coded message mistakenly identified the group as "two carriers and four heavy cruisers" situated 259 mi northwest of TF17. Based on this, Fletcher believed he had located the primary Japanese carrier group and commanded a full-scale aerial strike. By 10:13, 93 U.S. aircraft, including 18 Grumman F4F Wildcats, 53 Douglas SBD Dauntless dive bombers, and 22 Douglas TBD Devastator torpedo bombers, were airborne. Upon landing at 10:19, Nielsen realized his encoding mistake. While Gotō's force did feature the light carrier Shōhō, Nielsen had mistakenly identified two cruisers and four destroyers as the main fleet. By 10:12, Fletcher received information about an aircraft carrier and numerous other ships south of Nielsen's sighting. In reality, these B-17s had observed the same fleet as Nielsen: Shōhō, Gotō's cruisers, and the Port Moresby Invasion Fleet. Misinterpreting the B-17's discovery as the central Japanese carrier force (actually positioned much further east), Fletcher instructed the airborne strike team to engage this group.

At 09:15, Takahashi's aerial squadron arrived at their anticipated target location, identifying Neosho and Sims but spent several hours fruitlessly searching for the American carriers. It wasn't until 10:51 that the scout crew from Shōkaku recognized their error in misidentifying the oiler and destroyer duo as aircraft carriers. Takagi quickly surmised that the American carriers were positioned between his fleet and the invasion convoy, posing a significant threat to the Japanese invasion efforts. At 11:15, the torpedo bombers and their escorting fighters decided to abort the mission, returning to their carriers still carrying their munitions. Meanwhile, the 36 dive bombers targeted the two U.S. vessels.

Sims faced an assault from four of the dive bombers, receiving three direct hits. The severe damage caused the destroyer to split apart, rapidly sinking and resulting in the tragic loss of most of its crew, leaving only 14 survivors from its 192 personnel. Meanwhile, Neosho sustained hits from seven bombs, with one dive bomber, damaged by anti-aircraft fire, crashing into the oiler. Seriously impaired and powerless, Neosho was left adrift and gradually sinking. Though she managed to send a distress signal to Fletcher, the message was distorted, not clearly indicating the nature of the attack and providing incorrect coordinates for her location.

Meanwhile, the American strike force located Shōhō near Misima Island at 10:40 and prepared for their offensive. The Japanese carrier had a protective escort of six fighter aircraft, four Zeros and two Mitsubishi A5Ms, as the majority of its air fleet were being readied below deck for an impending assault on the American carriers. The carrier was further guarded by Gotō's cruisers, which positioned themselves around the carrier, forming a protective diamond pattern at a distance of 3,000–5,000 yd from each corner of Shōhō.

Lexington's air squad, under the command of William B. Ault, initiated the assault on Shōhō, landing two 1,000 lb bombs and five torpedoes, inflicting significant damage on the carrier. At 11:00, Yorktown's aerial team followed, bombarding the already aflame and nearly immobilized carrier with up to 11 additional 1,000 lb bombs and at least two torpedoes. The onslaught resulted in Shōhō's sinking at 11:35. Apprehensive about subsequent aerial attacks, Gotō directed his fleet northwards. However, he dispatched the destroyer Sazanami around 14:00 to save any survivors. From the carrier's initial crew of 834, only 203 were rescued. The attack cost the U.S. three aircraft: two SBDs from Lexington and another from Yorktown. Though all 18 of Shōhō's aircraft were destroyed, three pilots from the combat air patrol managed to safely land at Deboyne.

By 13:38, U.S. planes had safely returned and touched down on their respective carriers. By 14:20, the aircraft were prepped and equipped to strike either the Port Moresby Invasion Force or Gotō's fleet. With the locations of other Japanese fleet carriers still a mystery and intelligence suggesting the potential presence of up to four Japanese carriers supporting the MO operation,

Fletcher opted for caution. He reckoned that by the time his scouts located the remaining carriers, it would be too late to initiate a successful strike. Therefore, he decided against launching another strike that day, instead choosing to remain hidden under the dense cloud cover with fighters at the ready for defense, directing TF 17 towards the southwest.

In response to the loss of Shōhō, Inoue directed the invasion convoy to momentarily retreat northward and instructed Takagi, currently situated 259 mi east of TF 17, to neutralize the U.S. carrier forces. Though the retreating invasion convoy encountered bombing from eight U.S. Army B-17s, it evaded damage. Gotō and Kajioka received instructions to rally their fleets south of Rossel Island, preparing for a possible night surface engagement should the U.S. forces approach.

At 12:40, a seaplane originating from Deboyne identified and reported Crace's separate cruiser and destroyer group, noting its position as 90 mi from Deboyne on a 175° bearing. By 13:15, another aircraft from Rabaul spotted Crace's group but inaccurately reported it as containing two carriers, positioned 115 mi from Deboyne on a 205° bearing. Relying on these reports and still awaiting the return of his planes that had targeted Neosho, Takagi shifted his carriers due west at 13:30. At 15:00, he informed Inoue that he believed the U.S. carriers to be at a minimum distance of 490 mi west of his position, and as a result, an attack on them that day would not be feasible.

Two groups of attack aircraft from Rabaul, directed by Inoue's staff, headed towards Crace's position. The first group had 12 torpedo-armed G4M bombers, while the second had 19 Mitsubishi G3M aircraft with bombs. They attacked Crace's ships at 14:30, mistakenly claiming to have sunk and damaged battleships. However, Crace's ships were untouched and downed four G4Ms. Later, U.S. B-17s mistakenly bombed Crace without causing harm.

At 15:26, Crace informed Fletcher he needed air support and moved his ships 220 mi southeast of Port Moresby to avoid Japanese aircraft and stay near potential Japanese naval routes. With fuel running low and Fletcher maintaining silence, Crace was unsure of Fletcher's status.

Around 15:00, after receiving a faulty reconnaissance report, Zuikaku assumed Fletcher's carriers were nearing strike range. Despite the potential risks of a night return, Takagi and Hara decided to launch an immediate strike. Hara sent scouts to verify the U.S. carriers' location and, later, dispatched 27 aircraft towards them.

By 17:47, Task Force 17 detected the Japanese strike. U.S. Wildcats surprised the Japanese, downing eight aircraft. Heavy losses led the Japanese to cancel the mission. Some Japanese bombers mistakenly approached U.S. carriers in the dark but were driven away by anti-aircraft fire.

Meanwhile, Neosho transmitted distress signals indicating it was sinking, alerting Fletcher that his only nearby fuel source was lost.

As darkness set in, both sides adjusted their courses, planning their next moves. Fletcher and Crace decided to move westward. Inoue instructed Takagi to target the U.S. carriers, while the latter repositioned his ships northward. Gotō and Kajioka couldn't organize a nighttime assault on Allied ships.

On the morning of 8 May, at 06:15, Hara dispatched seven torpedo bombers from a location 100 nmi east of Rossel Island to scout the sector between 140–230° up to 250 nmi away. Assisting this effort were three Kawanishi H6Ks from Tulagi and four G4M bombers from Rabaul. By 07:00, the Japanese carrier strike group, now joined by Gotō's cruisers Kinugasa and Furutaka for added defense, veered southwest. Meanwhile, the invasion convoy and the other commanders positioned themselves 40 nmi east of Woodlark Island, awaiting the carrier battle's results. Overnight, a cloud front that had previously shielded the U.S. carriers now covered the Japanese fleet, restricting visibility to a range of 2-15 nmi.

Simultaneously, at 06:35, Task Force 17 (TF 17), under Fitch's tactical direction and located 180 nmi southeast of the Louisiades, sent out 18 SBDs for a comprehensive 360° search up to 200 nmi. The skies above the U.S. carriers remained mostly clear, offering a visibility of about 17 nmi.

By 08:20, an SBD from the Lexington, flown by Joseph G. Smith, identified the Japanese carriers through a gap in the cloud cover and informed TF 17. Just two minutes later, Kenzō Kanno, piloting a search plane from Shōkaku, spotted TF 17 and relayed this to Hara. The opposing forces were approximately 210 nmi apart. Both fleets hurriedly began launching their attack aircraft.

At 09:15, the Japanese carriers dispatched a combined strike force consisting of 18 fighters, 33 dive bombers, and 18 torpedo planes, led by Takahashi, with Shimazaki guiding the torpedo bombers. Meanwhile, the U.S. carriers initiated separate attacks. By 09:15, Yorktown had launched its team of six fighters, 24 dive bombers, and nine torpedo planes. Ten minutes later, Lexington sent out its group comprising nine fighters, 15 dive bombers, and 12 torpedo planes. Both U.S. and Japanese naval fleets raced towards each other, aiming to reduce the return flight distance for their aircraft.

Upon reaching the Japanese carriers at 10:32, Yorktown's dive bombers, under William O. Burch's leadership, waited for their torpedo squadron to catch up, aiming for a coordinated attack. At that moment, Shōkaku and Zuikaku were positioned approximately 10,000 yd apart, with Zuikaku obscured by a rain squall and low clouds. They were guarded by 16 CAP Zero fighters. The Yorktown dive bombers initiated their assault on Shōkaku at 10:57, managing to hit the carrier with two 1,000 lb bombs, inflicting significant damage to its forecastle and both flight and hangar decks. However, Yorktown's torpedo planes failed to achieve any hits. The skirmish resulted in the loss of two U.S. dive bombers and two CAP Zeros.

At 11:30, Lexington's aircraft entered the fray. Two of its dive bombers targeted Shōkaku, managing to strike it with a 1,000 lb bomb, exacerbating the carrier's damage. Another pair of dive bombers aimed at Zuikaku but failed to score any hits. The remaining dive bombers from Lexington struggled to locate the Japanese carriers amidst the dense clouds. Additionally, Lexington's torpedo planes were unsuccessful, with all 11 torpedoes missing Shōkaku. During this period, 13 CAP Zeros engaged in combat, downing three U.S. Wildcats.

Shōkaku was left in a dire state, with her flight deck severely compromised and 223 crew members either dead or injured. Additionally, she faced explosions in her gasoline storage and the destruction of an engine repair workshop, rendering her incapable of further aircraft operations. Captain Takatsugu Jōjima sought permission from Takagi and Hara to retreat from the battle. With their consent, Shōkaku, flanked by two destroyers, began its withdrawal to the northeast at 12:10.

At 10:55, Lexington's advanced CXAM-1 radar system picked up incoming Japanese aircraft, 78 mi away. In response, nine Wildcats were dispatched to counter the threat. However, having anticipated the Japanese torpedo bombers to be flying at a much lower altitude, six of the Wildcats were positioned too low, allowing the Japanese aircraft to fly over them without confrontation.

Due to significant aircraft losses from the previous night, the Japanese weren't equipped to launch a full-scale torpedo assault on both American carriers. Lieutenant Commander Shigekazu Shimazaki, leading the Japanese torpedo squad, directed 14 planes towards Lexington and the remaining four towards Yorktown. As the Japanese prepared their attack, a Wildcat downed one of their aircraft, while patrolling SBDs (eight from Yorktown and 15 from Lexington) took out three more. In retaliation, escorting Japanese Zeros eliminated four of Yorktown's SBDs. Notably, one of the surviving pilots, Swede Vejtasa, asserted that he had taken down three Zeros during the engagement, although records indicate no Zero losses.

At 11:13, the Japanese offensive commenced. With the carriers positioned 3,000 yd from each other, the fleets unleashed their anti-aircraft artillery. The quartet of torpedo planes targeting Yorktown failed to score a hit. In contrast, Lexington, which had a significantly wider turning radius compared to Yorktown, was subjected to a coordinated attack and sustained hits from two Type 91 torpedoes at 11:20. The first torpedo compromised the ship's port-side aviation fuel storage, inadvertently allowing gasoline fumes to seep into adjacent sections. The second strike disrupted the port water main, leading to reduced water pressure in the front firerooms and the consequent shutdown of associated boilers. Despite this, Lexington could still maintain a speed of 28 mph. Defensive anti-aircraft measures successfully took down four of the attacking Japanese torpedo planes.

The Japanese dive bombers waited to launch their offensive from an upwind position. Initiating their descent from 14,000 ft a few minutes post the torpedo attacks, the 19 dive bombers from Shōkaku, under Takahashi's command, set their sights on Lexington. The rest, led by Tamotsu Ema, went for Yorktown. While Takahashi's bombers were shielded from four of Lexington's CAP Wildcats by escorting Zeros, two Wildcats above Yorktown managed to disrupt Ema's formation. Lexington took two direct bomb hits and several close calls, igniting fires that were subdued by 12:33. Meanwhile, Yorktown suffered a hit at 11:27 from a single 250 kg semi-armour-piercing bomb that penetrated multiple decks, causing significant structural harm, casualties, and rendering some boilers unusable. Additionally, several near misses caused damage to Yorktown's underwater hull. Amidst the chaos, a CAP Wildcat succeeded in downing two of the attacking dive bombers.

After the Japanese aircraft finished their assaults and began their retreat, thinking they had critically damaged both carriers, they encountered a barrage of CAP Wildcats and SBDs. In the subsequent aerial skirmishes, the U.S. lost three SBDs and three Wildcats, while the Japanese saw three torpedo bombers, a dive bomber, and a Zero fall. By noon, aircraft from both the U.S. and Japanese forces were en route back to their carriers. On this journey back, planes from both sides crossed paths, leading to further aerial confrontations. Both Kanno and Takahashi met their end in these clashes, with their aircraft being taken down.

The returning aircraft, many showing signs of battle damage, made their landings on their respective carriers from 12:50 to 14:30. Despite their wounds, both the Yorktown and Lexington were capable of accepting aircraft from their air units. However, during these operations, the U.S. inadvertently lost another five SBDs, two TBDs, and a Wildcat, while the Japanese lost two Zeros, five dive bombers, and one torpedo bomber. Out of the initial 69 Japanese aircraft that were part of the strike force, 46 made it back to Zuikaku. Of these, several, including three Zeros, four dive bombers, and five torpedo planes, were deemed irreparable and were quickly discarded into the ocean.

As Task Force 17 carried out its recovery actions, Fletcher evaluated the prevailing circumstances. Reports from the returning pilots claimed one carrier was severely damaged while another seemed untouched. Observing the damages on his own carriers and noting significant fighter losses, coupled with concerns about fuel, especially after the Neosho's loss, he felt uneasy. By 14:22, Fitch had relayed intel suggesting the presence of two untouched Japanese carriers, a sentiment that radio intercepts supported. Given the supposed advantage of the Japanese in carrier capability, Fletcher chose to pull Task Force 17 out of the fray. He then sent coordinates of the Japanese carriers to MacArthur, hinting at a potential strike using his land-based bombers.

By 14:30, Hara had briefed Takagi, revealing that they only had 24 operational Zeros, eight dive bombers, and four torpedo planes. Fuel was another issue, with their cruisers at half capacity and certain destroyers nearing a critical 20%. At 15:00, Takagi relayed to Inoue their belief that two U.S. carriers, including the Yorktown and one of the "Saratoga-class," had been sunk. But, the considerable loss of aircraft meant that they couldn't maintain aerial cover for the planned invasion. Having earlier received intel on Crace's vessels, Inoue decided to call the invasion fleet back to Rabaul, pushing the

MO operation to 3 July, and marshaled his forces near the Solomons to initiate the RY operation. Zuikaku and her accompanying vessels moved towards Rabaul, while Shōkaku set a course for Japan.

On the Lexington, although the initial fires had been extinguished and the ship seemed operational, at 12:47, an unfortunate spark from neglected electric equipment ignited gasoline vapors near the ship's main control area. This blast claimed the lives of 25 crew members and sparked a raging fire. Subsequent explosions rocked the ship at 14:42 and 15:25. By 15:38, it became evident to the crew that the fires couldn't be tamed. Evacuation procedures began at 17:07. After ensuring all survivors, including Admiral Fitch and Captain Frederick C. Sherman, were safely off the ship, the destroyer Phelps was ordered to scuttle the burning vessel. At 19:15, Phelps launched five torpedoes into Lexington, which subsequently sank by 19:52 in deep waters at coordinates 15°15'S 155°35'E. Of the 2,951 crew members aboard, 216 perished along with 36 aircraft. The rescue ships promptly regrouped with the Yorktown and its convoy, which had left the scene at 16:01, moving Task Force 17 to a safer location in the southwest. Later in the night, MacArthur updated Fletcher, reporting that his B-17 bombers had targeted the retreating invasion convoy.

As night fell, Crace, facing concerns about the fuel status of Hobart and engine issues with the destroyer Walke, directed both vessels to head to Townsville. Even though he caught radio updates indicating the enemy's retreat, Crace, unaware of Fletcher's retreat, decided to keep Task Group 17.3 patrolling the Coral Sea. He was cautious of the possibility that the Japanese could redirect their invasion force towards Port Moresby.

On 9 May, Task Force 17 changed its direction eastward, taking a path south of New Caledonia out of the Coral Sea. After refueling at Tongatabu, Fletcher was instructed by Nimitz to promptly get Yorktown back to Pearl Harbor. That same day, U.S. Army bombers targeted Deboyne and Kamikawa Maru, but the extent of the damage was uncertain. Crace, having received no updates from

Fletcher, inferred that TF17 had left the vicinity. By 01:00 on 10 May, with no new reports of Japanese naval movement toward Port Moresby, Crace set course for Australia. He arrived at Cid Harbor, 240 km south of Townsville, on 11 May.

At 22:00 on 8 May, Yamamoto directed Inoue to reverse course, tackle any remaining Allied ships, and finalize the Port Moresby invasion. Although Inoue maintained the recall of the invasion convoy, he tasked Takagi and Gotō to chase down any residual Allied naval presence in the Coral Sea. Constrained by low fuel, Takagi's ships refueled from the Tōhō Maru throughout 9 May. By the night's end, Takagi and Gotō moved first southeast, then southwest into the Coral Sea. The following morning, Deboyne's seaplanes aided Takagi in his search for TF 17. However, Fletcher and Crace had already vacated the region. By 13:00 on 10 May, Takagi discerned that the opposition had retreated and began his journey back to Rabaul. Yamamoto agreed with this move and directed Zuikaku to Japan for air group replenishment. Concurrently, Kamikawa Maru left Deboyne. On 11 May at noon, a U.S. Navy PBY from Nouméa located the adrift Neosho. The U.S. destroyer Henley came to the rescue, saving 123 survivors from Neosho and Sims, and subsequently sank the tanker.

Operation RY initiated on 10 May. After the operation's flagship, the minelayer Okinoshima, was taken down by the U.S. submarine S-42 on 12 May, the landings were rescheduled to 17 May. Around this period, Halsey's TF 16 reached the South Pacific close to Efate. On 13 May, they moved north to counter the Japanese advancement to Nauru and Ocean Island. On 14 May, with intel about the Combined Fleet's impending operation against Midway, Nimitz commanded Halsey to ensure his ships were spotted by Japanese scouts the next day, and then immediately head back to Pearl Harbor. On 15 May, at 10:15, a Kawanishi scout plane from Tulagi spotted TF 16 east of the Solomons. Halsey's strategy succeeded. Concerned about a potential carrier air strike on his invasion units, Inoue promptly halted RY, recalling his fleet to Rabaul and Truk. By 19 May, after refueling near Efate, TF 16 made its way to Pearl

Harbor, arriving on 26 May. Yorktown docked a day later.

On 17 May, Shōkaku narrowly avoided capsizing during a storm due to her combat-inflicted damages as she made her way to Kure, Japan. A few days later, on 21 May, Zuikaku docked at Kure after making a short detour to Truk on 15 May. Relying on intelligence, the U.S. deployed eight submarines anticipating the carriers' return to Japan. However, these submarines didn't launch any attacks. The Japanese Naval General Staff projected a repair and replenishment timeline of two to three months for Shōkaku and the carriers' air groups. This meant that neither carrier would be available for Yamamoto's impending Midway campaign. By 14 July, both carriers were back with the Combined Fleet and played crucial roles in the ensuing naval clashes against the U.S. The five I-class submarines that initially supported the MO operation were redirected to launch an assault on Sydney Harbour in the subsequent weeks, aiming to hinder Allied logistical routes. As it was heading to Truk, the submarine I-28 encountered tragedy on 17 May; it was struck by a torpedo from the U.S. submarine Tautog and went down, claiming the lives of all on board.

Battle of Midway

Having initiated conflict in the Pacific's western frontiers, the Japanese Empire swiftly achieved its preliminary strategic objectives, capturing British Hong Kong, the Philippines, British Malaya, Singapore, and the Dutch East Indies (today's Indonesia). The Dutch East Indies, with its crucial oil reserves, held significant importance to Japan. As a result, early preparations for the next phase of operations began by January 1942.

Due to divergent strategic views between the Imperial Army (IJA) and Imperial Navy (IJN) and internal disputes within the Navy's Imperial General Headquarters and Admiral Isoroku Yamamoto's Combined Fleet, a subsequent strategy wasn't established until April 1942. Only after Yamamoto hinted at resignation did he win the internal tussle, leading to the adoption of his Central Pacific plan.

Yamamoto's primary objective was to neutralize America's carrier capabilities, which he saw as the primary obstacle to Japan's Pacific campaign. The Doolittle Raid on 18 April 1942 intensified this concern. During this operation, 16 USAAF B-25 Mitchell bombers, launched from the USS Hornet, struck Tokyo and other Japanese cities. Though the raid's military impact was minimal, it shocked the Japanese, exposing weaknesses in their homeland defenses and revealing their vulnerability to American air raids.

Further hit-and-run raids by U.S. carriers in the South Pacific emphasized their continued menace, even if they appeared hesitant for full-scale engagement. Yamamoto believed that another strike on Naval Station Pearl Harbor would lure the entire American fleet, including its carriers. Yet, given the bolstered American land-based air defenses on the Hawaiian Islands post the 7 December 1941 attack, he deemed a direct strike on Pearl Harbor too perilous.

Yamamoto then chose Midway, a small atoll on the northwest tip of the Hawaiian Island chain, roughly 2,100 km from Oahu. This placed Midway beyond the effective reach of most American aircraft based in the main Hawaiian Islands. While Midway wasn't a primary target in Japan's broader plans, they believed the U.S. would view it as a crucial extension of Pearl Harbor and therefore staunchly defend it. The U.S. indeed deemed Midway critical: post-battle, they established a submarine base there, enabling submarines from Pearl Harbor to refuel and extend their operational radius by 1,900 km. Besides being a seaplane base, Midway's runways also acted as an advanced launch point for bomber raids on Wake Island.

In line with the intricacies of Japanese naval strategies during World War II, Yamamoto's plan for capturing Midway, termed Operation MI, was notably intricate. The strategy hinged on the meticulous coordination of several battle groups across vast oceanic expanses. Furthermore, Yamamoto banked on faulty intelligence, assuming only the USS Enterprise and USS Hornet of Task Force 16 were at the Pacific Fleet's disposal. The preceding Battle of the Coral Sea had seen the sinking of the USS Lexington, and the USS Yorktown was believed to be lost due to severe damage. Yet, after swift repairs at Pearl Harbor, Yorktown played a pivotal role in detecting and eventually decimating the Japanese fleet carriers at Midway. Additionally, Yamamoto's strategy, reflective of the Japanese leadership's sentiment, underestimated American morale, which they presumed had waned due to consecutive Japanese triumphs.

Yamamoto believed subterfuge was essential to ensnare the U.S. fleet. Consequently, he scattered his forces to mask their full strength from the Americans. Notably, Yamamoto's support fleet of battleships and cruisers lagged hundreds of miles behind Admiral Chūichi Nagumo's carrier squad. They were strategized to finalize the annihilation of the U.S. fleet, weakened by Nagumo's carriers, in a daylight battle – a tactic standard in many significant navies then.

Unknown to Yamamoto, the U.S. had deciphered segments of the primary Japanese naval code (referred to as JN-25 by the Americans), which exposed his strategy. His emphasis on force dispersal also ensured his units couldn't mutually support. For example, while Nagumo's carriers were earmarked for Midway assaults and to absorb American retaliation, his fleet, beyond a dozen destroyers, consisted of just two Kongō-class fast battleships, two heavy cruisers, and one light cruiser. In contrast, forces under Yamamoto and Kondo had two light carriers, five battleships, four heavy cruisers, and two light cruisers, none of which participated in the Midway battle.

The slower speed of Yamamoto's light carriers and three battleships meant they couldn't accompany the Kidō Butai carriers. The Kidō Butai aimed for surprise by moving swiftly, without spreading its ships over vast distances. If other invasion segments required defense, the Kidō Butai would rush to their aid. This speed discrepancy meant slower ships couldn't accompany the Kidō Butai. This separation had severe repercussions during the battle, depriving Nagumo of the crucial reconnaissance from the scout planes on cruisers and carriers and additional anti-aircraft capabilities from the cruisers and other Kongō-class battleships.

To secure backing from the IJA for the Midway initiative, the IJN pledged support for their invasion of the U.S. through the Aleutian Islands, Attu and Kiska, situated within the organized Alaska Territory. The primary intent behind Japan's occupation of these islands was to push the U.S. land-based bombers stationed in Alaska out of striking range of the Japanese mainland. Conversely, a prevalent concern among Americans was that the Japanese would use these occupied territories as launching pads for bombing raids targeting vital sites and populated regions on the U.S. West Coast.

The Aleutian campaign (dubbed Operation AL) diverted additional ships that might have reinforced the Midway assault force. Contrary to earlier historical interpretations, which viewed the Aleutians operation as merely a diversion, the original Japanese strategy intended for Operation AL to commence in tandem with the Midway assault. However, a one-day delay in Nagumo's task force departure meant that Operation AL kicked off a day before the attack on Midway.

Facing a formidable enemy expected to deploy four or five carriers, Admiral Chester W. Nimitz, the Pacific Ocean Areas Commander in Chief, was in dire need of all available carriers. At his disposal was Vice Admiral William Halsey's task force, which boasted the carriers Enterprise and Hornet. However, due to Halsey being sidelined by shingles, Rear Admiral Raymond A. Spruance, Halsey's deputy, took command. Additionally, Nimitz urgently summoned Rear Admiral Frank Jack Fletcher and his task force, which included the carrier Yorktown, from the South West Pacific Area.

The Yorktown, having sustained damage during the Battle of the Coral Sea, was initially believed to need months of repair at the Puget Sound Naval Shipyard. Yet, its core components remained operational. The relentless efforts of the Pearl Harbor Naval Shipyard ensured the carrier was battle-ready within a mere 72 hours. Although it was expected to be operational for just a few weeks, this aligned with Nimitz's immediate needs. The carrier underwent extensive repair works, some of which continued even as she was deployed. Additionally, the USS Vestal, previously damaged during the Pearl Harbor attack, supplied onboard repair crews.

The Yorktown's air unit was replenished using any available aircraft and pilots. VS-5 was swapped for VB-3 from USS Saratoga, VT-5 was replaced by VT-3, and VF-3 was reformed, incorporating pilots from VF-42 and VF-3 under

Lieutenant Commander John S. "Jimmy" Thach. However, the inexperience among some crew members resulted in an unfortunate accident costing Lieutenant Commander Donald Lovelace his life. Even though there were attempts to ready the USS Saratoga, logistical challenges meant she arrived post-battle at Midway.

As for Midway, by June 4th, the U.S. Navy had positioned four PBY squadrons, totaling 31 aircraft for long-distance reconnaissance, and introduced six new Grumman TBF Avengers from the Hornet's VT-8. The Marine Corps had a mix of aircraft, including 19 Douglas SBD Dauntless, seven F4F-3 Wildcats, 17 Vought SB2U Vindicators, and 21 Brewster F2A Buffalos. The USAAF added 17 B-17 Flying Fortresses and four Martin B-26 Marauders equipped with torpedoes, culminating in 126 aircraft. Despite the F2As and SB2Us being outdated, they were all that was available for the Marine Corps.

A month prior, during the Battle of the Coral Sea, the Japanese light carrier Shōhō was destroyed. The fleet carrier Shōkaku suffered significant damage from three bomb hits and was in months-long repair. While fleet carrier Zuikaku emerged undamaged, she lost about half her air group. She was stationed in the Kure Naval District in Hiroshima awaiting replacements. The absence of immediate replacements highlighted the flaws in the IJN's pilot training program. Out of necessity, instructors from the Yokosuka Air Corps were reassigned as pilots.

Historians Jonathan Parshall and Anthony Tully suggest that Zuikaku could potentially have been fully equipped by pooling resources from both Shōkaku and herself. However, this would have been against Japanese carrier practices that emphasized carriers and their air groups training as unified entities. In contrast, the American system had a more flexible approach, allowing air squadrons to shift between carriers. It appears Japan didn't make significant efforts to prepare Zuikaku for the impending battle.

Consequently, Carrier Division 5, which had the Kido Butai's most advanced carriers, was unavailable. This left Vice-Admiral Nagumo with only four carriers: Kaga and Akagi in Carrier Division 1, and Hiryū and Sōryū in Carrier Division 2. A contributing factor was the operational fatigue the Japanese carriers had experienced since December 7, 1941, including raids on Darwin and Colombo. Nonetheless, the First Carrier Strike Force deployed with 248 aircraft across the four carriers.

Their primary carrier aircraft were the Aichi D3A1 "Val" dive bomber and the Nakajima B5N2 "Kate," serving as either a torpedo bomber or level bomber. The Mitsubishi A6M Zero was the main carrier fighter. Due to various reasons, "Val" production reduced drastically, and "Kate" production halted. Many of these aircraft, which had been in operation since late 1941, were nearing the end of their operational life, making them unreliable. This resulted in all Kido Butai carriers operating below their typical aircraft capacity, with limited spare parts.

Moreover, Nagumo's carriers had notable defensive shortcomings. Mark Peattie described them as having a "'glass jaw': they could strike but were vulnerable in return." Japanese carrier anti-aircraft capabilities were limited, and their combat air patrol had too few fighters and lacked an efficient early warning system, including radar. Their communication with fighter aircraft was subpar, and the escort ships were more scouts than close anti-aircraft escorts, lacking the requisite training and weaponry.

Additionally, Japanese pre-battle reconnaissance was disorganized. Their submarine picket line was late, allowing American carriers to approach Midway undetected. Another scouting attempt using H8K "Emily" flying boats was unsuccessful due to unexpected American presence in a previously deserted refueling bay. This left Japan uninformed about American carrier movements leading up to the battle.

Though Japanese radio intercepts identified increased American submarine and message activity, Yamamoto, aboard the Yamato, made no changes to the plan. While he received these messages, he mistakenly believed Nagumo had received the same, opting not to radio him to keep his location secret. Contrary to earlier beliefs, Nagumo did receive these messages before the battle. Why he chose not to adjust his strategy remains a mystery.

Nimitz held a crucial edge: U.S. codebreakers had made inroads into the Japanese Navy's JN-25b code. Since the start of 1942, they decrypted messages indicating an upcoming operation at target "AF." The exact location of "AF" was unclear until Commander Joseph Rochefort and the team at Station HYPO confirmed it to be Midway. They employed a strategy, orchestrated by Captain Wilfred Holmes, to have Midway send an uncoded message about a water system malfunction. Within a day, Japanese signals indicated "AF" was experiencing a water shortage. Surprisingly, no Japanese radio operators raised concerns about such a vital message being transmitted without encryption.

HYPO also pinpointed the attack date to be around 4 or 5 June and furnished Nimitz with detailed information on the Japanese forces. While Japan had updated its codebook, its implementation was postponed, allowing HYPO to continue decoding vital messages for several key days. Though Japan switched to the new code by 24 May, critical intel had already been obtained.

This intelligence gave the Americans a clearer understanding of the Japanese's planned movements and strengths. Nimitz was aware that the Japanese had diluted their strength by scattering their fleet into four distinct groups, spread out to the extent that mutual support was impossible. This configuration meant a limited number of swift ships could guard the Carrier Striking Force, thereby reducing the anti-aircraft defense around the carriers. Nimitz deduced that the U.S. could achieve a balance in air power against Yamamoto's four carriers, considering the larger size of American carrier air groups compared to the Japanese. On the other hand, the Japanese largely remained in the dark about the actual strength and positioning of the U.S. forces, even once the battle was underway.

Around 09:00 on 3 June, Ensign Jack Reid, flying a PBY from U.S. Navy's VP-44, identified the Japanese Occupation Force approximately 500 nmi west-southwest of Midway. However, he incorrectly labeled this as the Main Force. By midday, nine B-17s from Midway embarked on the first aerial assault, eventually locating Tanaka's transport group to the west. Under heavy anti-aircraft resistance, they launched their attack but, despite their claims, no real damage was inflicted.

In the early hours of the next day, a torpedo from a PBY made contact with the Japanese oil tanker Akebono Maru, marking the U.S.'s sole successful air-launched torpedo strike in the battle.

By dawn on 4 June, Nagumo initiated his first attack on Midway with a fleet of aircraft, simultaneously deploying seven reconnaissance planes. Japanese scouting was suboptimal due to limited aircraft and challenging weather. Concurrently, 11 PBYs took off from Midway for reconnaissance, with two subsequently detecting Japanese forces.

Midway's defenses were on alert, detecting the incoming attack from miles away and launching interceptors. As the U.S. bombers pursued the Japanese fleet, the defensive fighters stayed back to protect Midway. By 06:20, the Japanese attack had severely damaged the U.S. base. American defenses, led by Major Floyd B. Parks, faced heavy casualties but managed to down some Japanese aircraft. Of the Japanese fleet engaged, 11 planes were destroyed, with many more damaged. Still, the U.S. airbase at Midway remained functional, with Japanese pilots suggesting a subsequent strike was needed.

U.S. bombers, which had taken off before the Japanese assault, staged multiple raids on the Japanese carriers. This offensive involved various U.S. aircraft, including the newly debuted Avengers. The Japanese successfully repelled these strikes with minimal losses. Major Lofton R. Henderson, leading his novice SBD squadron, was among the casualties and was later honored with an airfield named after him.

A particularly daring moment came when Lieutenant James Muri's B-26 made a low-level strafing run on the Akagi, under heavy fire. Another B-26, piloted by Lieutenant Herbert Mayes, in a near-suicidal move, almost crashed into Akagi's bridge, narrowly avoiding it. Such audacious tactics might have influenced Nagumo's decision to launch another attack on Midway, against Yamamoto's directives.

Amid these aerial battles, the American submarine USS Nautilus found herself close to the Japanese fleet. After launching unsuccessful torpedo attacks on enemy ships, she had to repeatedly dive to evade aggressive escorts. The destroyer Arashi notably spent a significant time pursuing the Nautilus.

As part of Yamamoto's strategy for Operation MI, Nagumo kept half of his aircraft in reserve, which included two squadrons each of dive bombers and torpedo bombers. At the time, the dive bombers were not equipped with bombs, as per their operational protocol. The torpedo bombers were ready, in case they encountered U.S. naval vessels.

At 07:15, due to the earlier attacks from Midway and recommendations for a subsequent strike, Nagumo directed his reserve aircraft to be equipped with general-purpose bombs for land attacks. This rearming process had been ongoing for nearly 30 minutes when a scout plane from Tone, though late, reported sighting an American naval formation to the east at 07:40. However, the scout failed to detail the American fleet's makeup. It seems Nagumo may have only gotten this report by 08:00.

Nagumo, thrown into a dilemma, quickly changed his orders to re-equip the bombers and sought detailed information on the American fleet's composition. After some delay, the scout plane reported spotting one American carrier, part of Task Force 16. The whereabouts of the other carrier remained unknown.

Carrier Division 2's leader, Rear Admiral Tamon Yamaguchi, suggested that

Nagumo attack immediately with the available forces. However, Nagumo was constrained by the impending return of his aircraft from the Midway strike. These planes had to land soon, or they'd run out of fuel and crash into the ocean. Due to previous operations, the Japanese hadn't readied their reserve planes for an immediate launch.

The few planes on the Japanese decks at that moment were mostly defensive. Preparing the deck and launching aircraft would need at least half an hour. Launching them immediately meant some of the reserves would go into battle without proper equipment or potentially without fighter protection.

Japanese naval strategy typically favored launching full, coordinated strikes. Nagumo's conservative approach was in line with this doctrine. The fact that another American airstrike arrived around 07:53 further convinced him of the need for another strike on Midway. Ultimately, Nagumo chose to first allow his returning planes to land, then send out the reserve planes, now equipped with torpedoes.

Some argue that had Nagumo risked and launched the available planes around 07:45, he could have potentially crippled two American carriers. Also, having fuel-loaded planes on the ships was risky, and keeping them on decks was even more perilous. Regardless, by that time, the decisive American counter-strike was already en route. Even if Nagumo had acted differently, he couldn't have thwarted the incoming American assault.

The American fleet had initiated their aerial attack against the Japanese. Based on early morning sightings, Fletcher, who commanded from the Yorktown, instructed Spruance to strike the Japanese as soon as possible. Meanwhile, he kept Yorktown on standby in anticipation of other potential Japanese carriers.

Spruance, evaluating the situation, decided to proceed with the strike despite the distance to the target. The task of orchestrating the launch was entrusted to Halsey's Chief of Staff, Captain Miles Browning. Due to the necessity of launching aircraft into the wind, the carriers had to move away from the Japanese at a rapid pace. Browning proposed a launch at 07:00, which would allow the carriers to approach the Japanese fleet closely over the next hour. The first aircraft took off just after this time from the carriers Enterprise and Hornet. Fletcher started his attack from Yorktown around 08:00.

Both Fletcher and Yorktown's captain, Elliott Buckmaster, had gained invaluable experience during the Coral Sea battle. However, there wasn't adequate time to share this knowledge with the Enterprise and Hornet, which were initiating the first strike. Spruance prioritized speed, urging aircraft to head directly to their target, emphasizing the urgency to neutralize enemy carriers for their fleet's protection.

Interestingly, while the Japanese managed to dispatch 108 aircraft in a mere seven minutes, the Enterprise and Hornet took over an hour to send off 117. Spruance opted for immediate action over a coordinated attack. The American aircraft took off in separate groups, knowing this approach might lead to reduced impact and increased losses. But Spruance believed this continuous pressure would hinder the Japanese from orchestrating a counterattack, hoping to catch Nagumo off guard.

However, the American aircraft faced challenges in locating their target. Hornet's strike group, under Commander Stanhope C. Ring, deviated from the intended course, causing its dive bombers to miss the Japanese carriers. Yet, Torpedo Squadron 8 from Hornet, under Lieutenant Commander John C. Waldron, maintained the correct direction. Unfortunately, Hornet's 10 F4Fs ran out of fuel, resulting in a forced landing.

Waldron's squadron encountered the enemy carriers, launching their attack at 09:20. By 09:40, VF-6 from Enterprise joined the assault. However, their Wildcat fighter escorts lost their way and, running low on fuel, were forced to retreat. This left the 15 TBD Devastators from VT-8 unguarded. Tragically, all of them were downed without causing any harm to the enemy. Out of the 30 aircrews, only Ensign George H. Gay, Jr. survived. He managed to execute his torpedo strike on the carrier Sōryū, but it was skillfully dodged. Similarly, VT-6, headed by Lieutenant Commander Eugene E. Lindsey, faced significant losses with 9 out of 14 Devastators downed. Yorktown's VT-3 fared no better; they lost 10 of their 12 Devastators around 10:10, with no successful hits, partially due to the poor performance of their Mark 13 torpedoes. This battle marked the final combat use of the TBD Devastator.

The Japanese defense, equipped with swift Zeros, quickly neutralized the slow and inadequately armed TBDs. Although some TBDs managed to approach their targets closely, launching torpedoes and even strafing the enemy carriers, their efforts were in vain as the torpedoes either missed or malfunctioned. The American torpedoes' early wartime performance was notably unreliable. Many torpedoes missed their target, detonated prematurely, or even when hitting the target, failed to detonate. Surprisingly, higher-ranked Navy officers and the Bureau of Ordnance seemed to overlook why several torpedoes, launched in close proximity to the Japanese carriers, yielded no results.

While the American torpedo attacks didn't land any direct hits, they had three significant consequences. Firstly, they disrupted the Japanese carriers, hindering their ability to initiate a counterattack. Secondly, the Japanese Combat Air Patrol (CAP) was improperly positioned for the subsequent waves of attacks. Lastly, the continuous engagement drained many of the Zero fighters of their ammunition and fuel. By 10:00, when VT-3 from Yorktown launched another torpedo assault, most of the Japanese CAP was drawn to defend against it, leaving other areas vulnerable.

Coincidentally, as VT-3 made its move, three American SBD dive-bomber squadrons from Enterprise and Yorktown were closing in from different directions. The Yorktown squadron had chosen a unique attack route, while the two from Enterprise were running low on fuel after an extended search for the enemy fleet. However, fortune favored them when they noticed the Japanese destroyer Arashi's wake, which was rushing back to the main fleet after a skirmish with the U.S. submarine Nautilus. Some of the bombers, unfortunately, ran out of fuel before they could engage.

Admiral Chester Nimitz later praised McClusky's determination to extend the search, emphasizing its pivotal role in determining the outcome of the battle. The convergence of the three dive-bomber squadrons couldn't have been better timed or positioned. With most of the Japanese CAP distracted by VT-3, their carriers were in a vulnerable state: armed aircraft cluttered the hangar decks, fuel hoses were scattered due to rushed refueling, and the constant switching of ammunition meant bombs and torpedoes were hazardously placed around the hangars, instead of being secured. This situation left the Japanese fleet exceedingly exposed.

At 10:22, two squadrons from the Enterprise aimed to target the Japanese carriers Kaga and Akagi. Due to a miscommunication, both squadrons mistakenly targeted Kaga. Realizing the oversight, Lieutenant Richard Halsey Best, accompanied by his two wingmen, diverted from their descent on Kaga, believing it was already doomed, and rerouted to target Akagi. Kaga faced the brunt of the attack, enduring between three to five direct hits that inflicted severe damage and ignited multiple fires. One devastating bomb struck near the bridge, resulting in the death of Captain Jisaku Okada and the majority of the ship's high-ranking officers.

A few moments later, Best and his team targeted Akagi. Mitsuo Fuchida, the aviator who spearheaded the Pearl Harbor assault, was on board during the attack. Though Akagi was hit by only one bomb, the impact was catastrophic. The bomb hit near the center elevator, descending to the upper hangar deck and detonating amidst the ready-to-launch aircraft. Nagumo's chief aide, Ryūnosuke Kusaka, described the scene as "a raging inferno, with casualties everywhere. Aircraft were engulfed in bright flames and thick black smoke, making it impossible to control the blaze." Another nearby underwater explosion caused the flight deck to twist upwards in an unusual manner and severely damaged the rudder.

At the same time, Yorktown's VB-3, led by Lieutenant Max Leslie, attacked Sōryū, landing at least three hits that resulted in severe destruction. The ship was engulfed in flames as gasoline fires spread, and detonations from stacked ammunition and bombs intensified the blaze. VT-3 aimed at Hiryū, which was positioned closely to Sōryū, Kaga, and Akagi, but didn't manage to hit their target.

In a mere six minutes, both Sōryū and Kaga were fiercely burning from bow to stern. Although Akagi was hit by just one bomb, the ensuing fires grew uncontrollably, and eventually, the ship had to be forsaken. Nagumo, deeply affected, hesitated to leave Akagi but was eventually convinced by Kusaka. By 10:46, Nagumo shifted his command to the light cruiser Nagara. Remarkably, all three carriers stayed afloat for a while since they had mainly sustained above-water damage, except for Akagi's rudder, impaired by a nearby explosion. Initial optimism of possibly saving or towing Akagi back to Japan faded, leading to the eventual decision to abandon and scuttle all three carriers. During Kaga's destruction, the submarine Nautilus reappeared, launching three torpedoes. One hit Kaga without detonating. Eventually, the Japanese destroyer Hagikaze took down the burning Kaga.

The only remaining Japanese aircraft carrier, Hiryū, promptly launched a counteroffensive. Hiryū's initial strike group, which included 18 D3As and 6 Zeros, tracked the withdrawing American planes and engaged the first carrier they spotted, Yorktown. The carrier sustained damage from three bomb hits, creating a gaping hole in its deck, incapacitating all but one boiler, and destroying an anti-aircraft installation. This forced Fletcher to shift his command team to the heavy cruiser Astoria. However, within an hour, Yorktown's damage control units managed to temporarily mend the flight deck and reignite some boilers, enabling the ship to attain a speed of 22 mph and continue air operations. Signifying a reduced speed, Yorktown raised a flag indicating 5 knots. Moreover, Captain Buckmaster ordered the hoisting of a significantly large American flag on the foremast as a symbolic gesture. The attack resulted in the loss of thirteen D3As and three Zeros for the Japanese, with two Zeros retreating prematurely after facing resistance from returning Enterprise's SBDs.

An hour later, Hiryū sent out a second strike group, composed of ten B5Ns and six Zeros, to target Yorktown. The restoration efforts on Yorktown had been so remarkable that the incoming Japanese pilots mistakenly believed they were approaching a different, untouched carrier. The ensuing assault critically damaged Yorktown with two torpedo strikes, causing her to lose power and tilt severely to her port side. This wave of attack resulted in the loss of five B5Ns and two Zeros for the Japanese.

The false reports that they had sunk two American carriers from the two separate strikes bolstered Japanese spirits. The remaining aircraft were recovered by Hiryū. Despite their significant losses, the Japanese remained hopeful, believing they could muster enough aircraft for one final assault against what they presumed to be the last operational American carrier.

As the day neared its end, a scout from Yorktown located the Hiryū, leading Enterprise to dispatch a squadron of 24 dive bombers, which included aircraft from both Enterprise and Yorktown. Even though Hiryū was guarded by a fleet of Zero fighters, the American assault was successful, landing four or possibly five bombs on the carrier. This rendered Hiryū incapable of launching or operating aircraft. Though a separate strike from Hornet targeted the escort ships, it didn't achieve any significant hits. Hiryū, severely damaged and set aflame, was later abandoned, and despite initial hopes to salvage the ship, she eventually sank. Notably, Captain Yamaguchi and the ship's captain, Tomeo Kaku, chose to remain aboard, marking the loss of one of Japan's most esteemed carrier officers.

As night approached, both sides evaluated their situations and began planning their next moves. Admiral Fletcher, having to relinquish the badly damaged Yorktown, transferred operational command to Admiral Spruance. Though aware of the significant American victory, Spruance remained cautious of remaining Japanese forces, ensuring both Midway and the American carriers were protected. As the night progressed, he shifted his position to avoid potential night battles with Japanese ships. Meanwhile, Admiral Yamamoto, hoping to continue the confrontation, dispatched his remaining ships to locate the American fleet. However, when no contact was made, he ordered a general withdrawal.

Spruance's cautious approach proved advantageous. If he had engaged with Yamamoto's superior fleet, particularly under the cover of night, it could have been disastrous for the American side given the Japanese naval prowess in nighttime warfare.

On June 5th, despite thorough searches, Spruance couldn't locate Yamamoto's forces. Later in the day, he sent out a mission to find and engage any remnants of Nagumo's carriers. While this mission didn't achieve its primary objective, upon returning after dark, Spruance made the decision to have Enterprise and Hornet illuminate their decks to aid in the safe landing of aircraft.

On the morning of 5 June, the submarine Tambor, commanded by John Murphy and located 90 nautical miles west of Midway, identified several unidentified vessels. Both Murphy and his executive officer, Edward Spruance (Admiral Spruance's son), were unable to confirm the identity of these ships. Instead of getting a closer look, Murphy relayed a vague report about "four large ships" to his superior. This report reached Admiral Spruance, who was left frustrated due to its lack of clarity. With no precise knowledge about the location of Yamamoto's main force, Spruance had to operate on the assumption that Tambor's sighting was the primary invasion force, so he positioned his fleet northeast of Midway accordingly.

In fact, the ships spotted were a detachment sent by Yamamoto to bombard

Midway. Around the time they altered course based on Yamamoto's orders, they sighted Tambor. In the ensuing maneuvers to avoid a potential submarine attack, two Japanese cruisers, Mogami and Mikuma, collided. By dawn, Murphy was finally able to ascertain that the ships were Japanese. His subsequent attack was unsuccessful, and his late and ambiguous report of two Mogami-class cruisers headed westward was his last contribution to the battle. Due to Murphy's unsatisfactory performance, upon Tambor's return to port, Spruance had him reassigned. Over the following days, the damaged Mogami and Mikuma were targeted by multiple air raids. While Mikuma was sunk, Mogami managed to limp back for repairs. In one of the strikes, U.S. Marine Corps aviator Captain Richard E. Fleming died during an attack run on Mikuma and received the Medal of Honor posthumously.

In parallel, there were promising salvage efforts on the damaged Yorktown, and the USS Vireo began towing her. However, on the afternoon of 6 June, the Japanese submarine I-168 penetrated the protective destroyer screen. It launched torpedoes, hitting Yorktown and the destroyer USS Hammann. Hammann, laden with depth charges, split in two and sank, resulting in significant loss of life. With Yorktown's condition deteriorating and salvage looking futile, the remaining crews were evacuated. Yorktown lingered through the night, but by the morning of 7 June, she had tilted significantly. By the early morning, the carrier capsized and eventually sank.

As the dust settled from the battle, Japanese losses were staggering, with a total of 3,057 lives lost. The breakdown of casualties among the carriers was as follows: Akagi suffered 267 deaths, Kaga had 811, Hiryū lost 392 (including Yamaguchi who made the decision to go down with the ship), and Soryū had 711 casualties, including Captain Yanagimoto who also chose to remain onboard, totaling 2,181 from the carriers alone. The heavy cruiser casualties included 700 from the sunken Mikuma and 92 from the severely damaged Mogami, amounting to another 792 lives lost.

Other damages during the air strikes that targeted Mikuma and further hit Mogami included the destroyers Arashio, with 35 casualties due to bombing, and Asashio, with 21 casualties from aerial strafing. Additionally, cruisers Chikuma and Tone lost three and two floatplanes, respectively. The remaining casualties came from the destroyers Tanikaze (11 deaths), Arashi (1), Kazagumo (1), and the fleet oiler Akebono Maru, which had 10 casualties.

On the U.S. side, the battle claimed the aircraft carrier Yorktown and the destroyer Hammann. The U.S. death toll reached 307, a number that included Major General Clarence L. Tinker, Commander of the 7th Air Force. Tinker had personally led a bombing raid against the retreating Japanese forces on June 7th, but tragically lost his life when his plane crashed near Midway Island.

After achieving a decisive victory, the American forces, cautious of approaching too close to Wake Island, began to pull back. Spruance retreated eastward to refuel the destroyers and to join up with the carrier Saratoga, which was on its way with crucial replacement aircraft. On the afternoon of 8 June, Fletcher moved his flag to Saratoga, taking back command of the carrier fleet. Over the next two days, Fletcher dispatched search missions from the carriers, ensuring that no Japanese forces were advancing towards Midway. By 10 June, they decided to depart the area, and eventually, the American carriers made their way back to Pearl Harbor.

Historical accounts highlight that Spruance faced criticism for not chasing the retreating Japanese, thereby letting their naval forces slip away. Blair, in 1975, contended that had Spruance pursued, he would have faced challenges in launching aircraft after dusk, and his cruisers might have been outmatched by the superior Japanese surface units, including the formidable Yamato. Additionally, the U.S. had suffered significant air group losses, rendering it unlikely they could effectively strike the Japanese battleships in daylight. Fuel shortages in Spruance's destroyers further complicated the situation.

On 10 June, the Japanese military conveyed an incomplete account of the battle's outcome. By 15 June, Nagumo had presented a detailed battle report, intended for only the top tiers of the Japanese Navy and leadership. Inter-estingly, the report assumed that the Americans were unaware of Japanese plans until 5 June. In truth, American code-breakers had compromised the operation from its inception.

The Japanese public and a significant portion of its military hierarchy were misinformed about the severity of the defeat, with the media proclaiming a significant victory. Only Emperor Hirohito and top Navy officials were apprised of the actual losses. The Japanese Army was led to believe, at least momentarily, that the fleet remained in a robust state.

When the Japanese fleet reached Hashirajima on 14 June, the injured were swiftly relocated to naval hospitals. Classified as "secret patients," they were isolated to conceal the extent of the defeat. Officers and crew who remained were promptly redistributed to other fleet units and sent to the South Pacific, where many met their fate in combat. High-ranking officials and staff faced no penalties, and Nagumo even assumed command of the revamped carrier force later on. It's worth noting that one reason Nagumo might have retained his position was his report indicating two American carriers had been destroyed, rather than the actual count of one.

Following the setback, the Japanese navy made several operational changes. More aircraft were now refueled and rearmed on the flight deck rather than in the hangars. Additionally, the procedure of emptying unused fuel lines became standard practice. Newly constructed carriers were modified to feature just two flight deck elevators and enhanced firefighting equipment. There was a concerted effort to train more carrier personnel in damage control and firefighting. However, the eventual loss of carriers like Shōkaku, Hiyō, and notably Taihō indicated lingering challenges in these areas.

To promptly replenish their pilot ranks, the navy hastened their training programs, compromising on quality. These novice pilots were sent to front-line units, burdening the surviving veterans from earlier battles like Midway and the Solomons. These seasoned pilots faced increasing demands without adequate rest, either in rear bases or back in Japan. Consequently, the proficiency of Japanese naval air squads waned over the course of the war, while their American counterparts only grew stronger.

Battle of Guadalcanal

On December 7, 1941, Pearl Harbor in Hawaii faced a surprise assault by Japanese forces. This unexpected strike resulted in the deaths of nearly 2,500 individuals and severely hampered the U.S. battleship fleet. Consequently, a formal war declaration ensued between the two nations the subsequent day. Japan's primary objectives included incapacitating the U.S. Navy, capturing resource-rich territories, and establishing fortified military bases to safeguard its Pacific and Asian empire. In quick succession, Japanese forces occupied territories including the Philippines, Thailand, Malaya, and more.

The Japanese initiated two significant offensives aiming to expand their defensive boundaries to places like Australia, Hawaii, and the U.S. mainland. The first of these offensives was stymied during the naval Battle of the Coral Sea, which, despite being tactically inconclusive, strategically favored the Allies. This battle marked the Allies' inaugural major victory against Japan, weakening their carrier strike capabilities. However, Japan's aggressive strategy remained unchanged for several pivotal months, evident in their unsuccessful assault on Port Moresby via the Kokoda track. Their second major push was halted at the Battle of Midway. These Allied triumphs shifted the balance of power, allowing them to go on the offensive against Japan.

The Allies pinpointed the Solomon Islands, specifically Guadalcanal, Tulagi, and Florida Island, for their first major operation. Interestingly, Guadalcanal, which later became central to the operation, was initially an afterthought, only gaining prominence when a Japanese airbase construction was discovered there. The Japanese had already occupied Tulagi by May and had started building an airfield on Guadalcanal by July. These moves alarmed the Allies, as Japanese bombers operating from such bases could threaten key supply routes.

The conception of the invasion plan for the southern Solomons came from U.S. Admiral Ernest King. The aim was to block the Japanese from using these islands as launch points and to safeguard supply routes between the U.S. and Australia. Although the primary focus was on defeating Germany, the Pacific front still competed for resources and personnel. Deciding who would lead the campaign posed another challenge, with jurisdictional overlaps between General Douglas MacArthur and Admiral Chester W. Nimitz. Eventually, after some adjustments, the operation received full backing, with the U.S. Navy assuming the main responsibility.

The overarching strategy for 1942-1943, as set by Chief of Staff William D. Leahy, emphasized capturing Guadalcanal, launching an Allied offensive in New Guinea under MacArthur, and targeting the Japanese stronghold at Rabaul. The ultimate goal was the U.S. reclaiming the Philippines. The South Pacific theater was established to oversee the Solomon's campaign, with Vice Admiral Robert L. Ghormley at its helm. Meanwhile, Nimitz, positioned at Pearl Harbor, was named the chief Allied commander for Pacific forces.

In May 1942, as part of the Pacific offensive preparations, U.S. Marine Major General Alexander Vandegrift received instructions to relocate his 1st Marine Division from the U.S. to New Zealand. Concurrently, various Allied naval, land, and air units were dispatched to either bolster or establish bases in locations such as Fiji, Samoa, New Hebrides, and New Caledonia.

The Allies chose Espiritu Santo in New Hebrides as the central headquarters and primary base for the upcoming operation, named Operation Watchtower, scheduled to begin on 7 August. Originally, the offensive was primarily aimed at Tulagi and the Santa Cruz Islands, excluding Guadalcanal. However, upon uncovering Japanese airfield developments on Guadalcanal, the Allies modified their strategy to include its capture, while the Santa Cruz initiative was eventually shelved. Despite noticing considerable Allied troop movements via signals intelligence, the Japanese mistakenly assumed that the Allies were strengthening their positions in Australia and possibly Port Moresby in New Guinea.

Assembling near Fiji on 26 July, the Watchtower force, comprising 75 warships and transport vessels from both the U.S. and Australia, undertook a single mock landing exercise. They set course for Guadalcanal on 31 July. The expedition's leadership fell to U.S. Vice Admiral Frank Fletcher, with his flag on the aircraft carrier USS Saratoga. U.S. Rear Admiral Richmond K. Turner was in charge of the amphibious operations, while Vandegrift led the 16,000-strong Allied infantry, predominantly U.S. Marines, designated for the landing. These troops, recently out of training and equipped with bolt-action M1903 Springfield rifles, had a scant 10-day ammunition supply. Operational constraints led to a reduction in their supply duration from the standard 90 days to a mere 60. Given this precarious situation, the 1st Marine Division humorously dubbed the upcoming conflict "Operation Shoestring".

The Allied forces, benefiting from adverse weather conditions, stealthily approached their target on the night of 6 August. The inclement conditions cloaked their arrival, enabling them to catch the Japanese defenders off guard in what's occasionally referred to as the "Midnight Raid on Guadalcanal". While a Japanese patrol plane from Tulagi did scout the vicinity where the Allied invasion fleet was advancing, it failed to spot them due to the heavy cloud cover and storms. Upon reaching their destination, the landing force divided into two groups, with one targeting Guadalcanal and the other focusing on Tulagi, Florida, and adjacent islands. Allied naval vessels unleashed a barrage on the landing areas, and U.S. aircraft from carriers targeted Japanese positions on the islands. This offensive neutralized 15 Japanese seaplanes stationed near Tulagi.

The islands of Tulagi, Gavutu, and Tanambogo came under assault from 3,000 U.S. Marines led by Brigadier General William Rupertus. The Japanese naval force of 886 personnel, responsible for the seaplane bases on these islands, mounted a tenacious defense against the Marines. Nonetheless, after intense combat, the Marines managed to secure all three islands: capturing Tulagi by 8 August and both Gavutu and Tanambogo by the next day. The Japanese defense was fierce, with nearly all of their personnel perishing in the battle, while the Marines reported 248 casualties.

The landing on Guadalcanal stood in stark contrast to the heavy resistance encountered on Tulagi, Gavutu, and Tanambogo. At 09:10 on 7 August, Vandegrift, leading 11,000 U.S. Marines, initiated a beach landing between Koli Point and Lunga Point on Guadalcanal. They progressed toward Lunga Point with minimal opposition and successfully secured the airstrip by the afternoon of 8 August. The Japanese naval units and combat personnel, headed by Captain Kanae Monzen, were forced to retreat due to the intense naval and aerial onslaught. They withdrew approximately 3 miles westward to the vicinity of the Matanikau River and Point Cruz, deserting valuable equipment, supplies, and 13 of their comrades.

While the landings progressed on 7 and 8 August, Japanese aircraft from Rabaul, under Yamada Sadayoshi's leadership, carried out multiple assaults on the Allied landing forces. Their strikes led to the ignition of transport vessel USS George F. Elliott, which eventually sank, and inflicted significant damage on the destroyer USS Jarvis. Over these two days, the Japanese lost 36 planes, while the U.S. saw a loss of 19, attributed to both combat and accidents, including 14 from carriers.

Following these aerial engagements, Fletcher grew concerned about the diminishing strength of his carrier fighter aircraft. He was also wary of potential Japanese aerial threats to his carriers and the decreasing fuel reserves. Consequently, Fletcher chose to pull his carrier groups from the Solomon Islands vicinity on the night of 8 August. The absence of air support from the carriers prompted Turner to make the tough decision to retreat with his ships from Guadalcanal, despite the fact that a significant portion of the essential supplies and equipment had yet to be offloaded. However, Turner intended to offload as much as possible on both Guadalcanal and Tulagi during the night of 8 August, planning to exit with his fleet early on 9 August.

During the evening of 8–9 August, as the transports were offloading, two groups of Allied cruisers and destroyers led by British Rear Admiral Victor Crutchley were caught off guard and bested by a Japanese force consisting of seven cruisers and one destroyer from the 8th Fleet stationed at Rabaul and Kavieng. This force was under the leadership of Japanese Vice Admiral Gunichi Mikawa.

The confrontation resulted in the sinking of one Australian and three American cruisers, while another American cruiser and two destroyers sustained damages. On the Japanese side, one cruiser experienced moderate damage. Unaware of Fletcher's plans to pull out with the U.S. carriers, Mikawa immediately retreated to Rabaul, opting not to engage the transports. He was apprehensive about potential U.S. carrier air strikes during daylight if he remained nearby. With the absence of his carrier air support, Turner chose to evacuate his remaining naval assets by the night of 9 August. This left the Marines on land with a significant amount of their equipment, supplies, and personnel still on the transports. Mikawa's choice to forego attacking the vulnerable Allied transport ships when he had the chance turned out to be a pivotal strategic oversight.

Upon landing on Guadalcanal, the 11,000-strong Marine force prioritized setting up a defensive ring around Lunga Point and the airfield, relocating the delivered supplies into this area, and finalizing the airfield's construction. Over a span of four days, they efficiently relocated supplies from the beach to secure storage sites within their defensive zone. The airfield's construction was expedited with the help of seized Japanese machinery. By the 12th of August, it was christened Henderson Field in honor of Lofton R. Henderson, a Marine pilot who fell during the Battle of Midway. Operational status was achieved by 18 August. Although the Marines managed to secure food for five days from the transport vessels, along with the provisions they found that belonged to the Japanese, they only had a total food supply that would last 14 days. This led to rationing, limiting the Marines to two meals each day.

Health challenges soon emerged as a significant number of Marines, nearly one-fifth by mid-August, fell ill with a potent strain of dysentery. While a handful of the Korean laborers gave themselves up to the Marines, the majority of the remaining Japanese and Korean personnel regrouped just west of the Lunga defensive line, near the Matanikau River's western bank, relying mostly on coconuts for sustenance. Another Japanese naval unit was situated at Taivu Point, approximately 22 miles to the east of the Lunga defensive zone. On 8 August, a Japanese destroyer arriving from Rabaul brought in 113 naval troops to reinforce the Matanikau position.

On the night of 12 August, a reconnaissance patrol made up of 25 U.S. Marines, under the command of Lieutenant Colonel Frank Goettge and largely comprising intelligence staff, embarked west of the Marine-held Lunga area. Situated between Point Cruz and the Japanese-held region near the Matanikau River, they aimed to gather intel and also establish contact with a Japanese faction that was suspected of being open to surrendering. However, shortly after their landing, they were ambushed by a Japanese naval platoon, resulting in significant casualties.

In retaliation, Vandegrift dispatched three companies from the U.S. 5th Marine Regiment on 19 August to confront the Japanese forces west of the Matanikau. The strategic assault involved one company attacking across the Matanikau River's sandbar, another launching an inland attack on Matanikau village, and the third striking Kokumbuna village from the west. Despite momentarily securing both villages, the Marine detachments retreated to the Lunga zone, having inflicted approximately 65 casualties on the Japanese and suffering a loss of four of their own. This encounter, often dubbed the "First Battle of the Matanikau", set the stage for subsequent significant clashes in the same vicinity during the campaign.

On 20 August, the escort carrier USS Long Island bolstered Henderson Field's air strength by delivering 19 Grumman F4F Wildcats and 12 Douglas SBD Dauntlesses. These aircraft, stationed at Henderson, earned the moniker "Cactus Air Force", drawing from the Allied codename for Guadalcanal. The very next day, these Marine fighter planes countered the inaugural strike of the frequent Japanese bombing raids. By 22 August, an additional reinforcement of five U.S. Army Bell P-400 Airacobras, along with their pilots, joined the forces at Henderson Field.

On the night of 12 August, a reconnaissance patrol made up of 25 U.S. Marines, under the command of Lieutenant Colonel Frank Goettge and largely comprising intelligence staff, embarked west of the Marine-held Lunga area. Situated between Point Cruz and the Japanese-held region near the Matanikau River, they aimed to gather intel and also establish contact with a Japanese faction that was suspected of being open to surrendering. However, shortly after their landing, they were ambushed by a Japanese naval platoon, resulting in significant casualties.

In retaliation, Vandegrift dispatched three companies from the U.S. 5th Marine Regiment on 19 August to confront the Japanese forces west of the Matanikau. The strategic assault involved one company attacking across the Matanikau River's sandbar, another launching an inland attack on Matanikau village, and the third striking Kokumbuna village from the west. Despite momentarily securing both villages, the Marine detachments retreated to the Lunga zone, having inflicted approximately 65 casualties on the Japanese and suffering a loss of four of their own. This encounter, often dubbed the "First Battle of the Matanikau", set the stage for subsequent significant clashes in the same vicinity during the campaign.

On 20 August, the escort carrier USS Long Island bolstered Henderson Field's air strength by delivering 19 Grumman F4F Wildcats and 12 Douglas SBD Dauntlesses. These aircraft, stationed at Henderson, earned the moniker "Cactus Air Force", drawing from the Allied codename for Guadalcanal. The very next day, these Marine fighter planes countered the inaugural strike of the frequent Japanese bombing raids. By 22 August, an additional reinforcement of five U.S. Army Bell P-400 Airacobras, along with their pilots, joined the forces at Henderson Field.

While the battle at Tenaru was winding down, the Japanese were already mobilizing additional reinforcements. Yamamoto assembled a formidable expeditionary force, with intentions not only to obliterate any American naval presence but also to reclaim Henderson Field. This force set out from Truk on 23 August, and multiple reinforcement and bombardment detachments departed both from Truk and Rabaul in tandem. On 16 August, three transport vessels left Truk, transporting the remainder of Ichiki's 28th Infantry Regiment and 500 naval marines from the 5th Yokosuka Special Naval Landing Force. These were safeguarded by a fleet of 13 warships under Japanese Rear Admiral Raizō Tanaka, with plans to reach Guadalcanal by 24 August.

To bolster this offensive, Yamamoto commissioned Chūichi Nagumo to lead a carrier contingent from Truk on 21 August, directing them towards the southern Solomon Islands. This force boasted three carriers and an armada of 30 additional ships. Yamamoto's strategy involved using the light carrier Ryūjō as potential bait, hoping it would distract American pilots while the two main carriers would initiate their attack.

Meanwhile, U.S. carriers, overseen by Fletcher, neared Guadalcanal to oppose the Japanese. On 24 August, a massive aerial showdown ensued between the forces. The U.S., with their carriers Saratoga and Enterprise, faced off against the Japanese fleet carriers Shōkaku and Zuikaku and the light carrier Ryūjō. While the Ryūjō took severe damage and ultimately sank, the Enterprise was also damaged, but both fleets ultimately withdrew. In this confrontation,

Japan lost the Ryūjō and a significant number of aircraft and crew, whereas the U.S. only lost a few aircraft.

Tanaka's convoy, led by flagship Jintsū, was ambushed near Taivu Point on 25 August by aircraft from Henderson Field. The assault inflicted considerable damage, causing the convoy to reroute to the Shortland Islands, where survivors were loaded onto destroyers for subsequent transport to Guadalcanal. In the wake of this skirmish, Japanese forces initiated an aerial assault on Guadalcanal, while the American carrier Wasp stood by east of the island, awaiting potential Japanese maneuvers.

From a strategic vantage point, this was a missed golden opportunity for the Japanese to clinch a game-changing victory. Instead, they inadvertently provided the Americans with a semblance of triumph. Furthermore, the bolstering of Henderson Field with aircraft from the Enterprise set a new operational standard, impeding Japanese daytime supply runs to Guadalcanal. What was once uncontested Japanese control of this marine territory was now restricted to nighttime operations.

For a duration of six weeks following the Battle of Savo Island until the end of September, the U.S. Navy's major warships and standard destroyers were given explicit orders to steer clear of Tulagi and Guadalcanal. This was due to apprehensions stemming from the severe losses experienced at Savo Island. During this period, the primary U.S. naval presence in the Ironbottom Sound was Transport Division 12. This fleet was composed of six aged Wickes-class destroyers from World War I, which had been repurposed as high-speed transports. These vessels underwent modifications, such as the removal of torpedo tubes, to accommodate over 100 additional Marines for swift deployment. These ships played pivotal roles, from landing the inaugural Marines on Tulagi and Guadalcanal, undertaking special ops with Marine Raiders, countering submarines, and offering fire support for the Marines on the island. Furthermore, they were instrumental in ferrying vital supplies, pivotal for the establishment and maintenance of Henderson Field.

A tragic event transpired on 30 August when the USS Colhounwas targeted by Japanese bombers, displaying impressive precision. The ship was lost along with 51 of its crew. Subsequently, on the night of 4–5 September, while the USS Little and USS Gregory were redeploying their Marine Raiders back to Guadalcanal and patrolling for enemy submarines, they encountered three Japanese destroyers. Initially mistaking them for submarines, the two American ships soon found themselves in a vulnerable position. Adding to the confusion, a U.S. patrol aircraft misidentified the scene and unintentionally spotlighted the American ships with flares, making them easy targets for the superior Japanese destroyers. In the ensuing battle, both Little and Gregory were sunk. Tragically, 65 men from the Little and 24 from the Gregory perished, including the commanding officers of both vessels and the head of Transport Division 12.

During August, Henderson Field on Guadalcanal saw a steady influx of U.S. aircraft along with their crews. By month's end, 64 aircraft of diverse types had been deployed there. U.S. Marine Brigadier General Roy Geiger, commander of the 1st Marine Aircraft Wing, arrived on 3 September with his staff, subsequently taking charge of all aerial operations out of Henderson Field. The skies above the island witnessed frequent dogfights between the Allied aircraft based at Henderson and Japanese bomber and fighter planes launching from Rabaul. From 26 August to 5 September, the U.S. faced a loss of around 15 aircraft compared to the Japanese loss of roughly 19. Remarkably, over half of the downed U.S. pilots were rescued, whereas most of the Japanese pilots weren't as fortunate. The considerable distance of about 1,120 miles for a round-trip flight between Rabaul and Guadalcanal posed a significant challenge for Japanese attempts to dominate the skies over Henderson Field. Valuable intelligence from Australian coastwatchers stationed on Bougainville and New Georgia islands often alerted the Allied forces on Guadalcanal about incoming Japanese aerial raids. This heads-up allowed U.S. fighter planes ample time to launch and strategically position themselves to counter the approaching Japanese. Over time, the Japanese air strength started dwindling in this attritional air war.

Simultaneously, on the ground, Vandegrift emphasized fortifying the Lunga perimeter's defenses. From 21 August to 3 September, he reallocated three Marine battalions from Tulagi and Gavutu to Guadalcanal, enhancing the defense force by around 1,500 troops. One of these units, the 1st Parachute Battalion, which had experienced heavy losses in the prior battles at Tulagi and Gavutu-Tanambogo, was now under Edson's leadership.

Another moved unit, the 1st Battalion, 5th Marine Regiment, was deployed by boat on 27 August west of the Matanikau. Their mission mirrored the earlier Matanikau action, intending to confront Japanese forces. However, challenging terrain and fortified Japanese defenses stalled their advance. By the following day, the Japanese forces had retreated overnight, leading the Marines to return to the Lunga perimeter. This operation resulted in 20 Japanese and 3 Marine casualties.

Allied naval convoys periodically reached Guadalcanal between late August and early September, bringing essential supplies to the Marines stationed at Lunga. These supplies included food, ammunition, aircraft fuel, technicians, and on 1 September, 392 Seabees who would work on maintaining and enhancing Henderson Field. Furthermore, starting 3 September, the Marine Aircraft Group 25 initiated air transport operations, delivering high-priority cargo, which encompassed personnel, fuel, ammunition, and other vital resources, to Henderson Field.

By the 23rd of August, Kawaguchi's 35th Infantry Brigade arrived at Truk and boarded slow-moving transport vessels destined for Guadalcanal. However, after witnessing the destruction of Tanaka's convoy during the Battle of the Eastern Solomons, the Japanese began to rethink their strategy of using slow transports for delivering troops. As a result, the vessels carrying Kawaguchi's brigade were rerouted to Rabaul. From there, the plan was to send these soldiers to Guadalcanal using destroyers that would pass through a Japanese naval base in the Shortland Islands. These Japanese destroyers typically managed to cover the distance down "The Slot" (New Georgia Sound) to

Guadalcanal and return in one night, reducing their vulnerability to Allied aerial bombardment. The Allies dubbed these trips the "Tokyo Express," while the Japanese called them "rat transportation." However, there was a limitation: while troops could be transported this way, heavy equipment like artillery, vehicles, and significant supplies couldn't. Additionally, the Japanese fleet's commitment to this strategy strained the destroyers that were critically required to safeguard other convoys. The Allies, whether due to constraints or choice, seldom contested Japanese naval supremacy at night. This meant the Japanese effectively controlled the waters surrounding the Solomon Islands after sunset. Yet, during the day, any Japanese vessel within 200 miles of the aircraft stationed at Henderson Field was highly vulnerable to airstrikes. This dynamic remained for several months of the campaign.

From the 29th of August to the 4th of September, the Japanese managed to land nearly 5,000 troops at Taivu Point. This included the majority of the 35th Infantry Brigade, a significant portion of the Aoba (4th) Regiment, and the remnants of Ichiki's regiment. On the Tokyo Express run on 31st August, General Kawaguchi arrived at Taivu Point, subsequently taking charge of all Japanese troops in Guadalcanal. Another group, comprising 1,000 soldiers from Kawaguchi's brigade and led by Colonel Akinosuke Oka, reached Kamimbo, west of the Lunga perimeter, via a barge convoy.

On the 7th of September, Kawaguchi detailed his assault strategy to decisively "eliminate the adversary near the Guadalcanal Island airstrip." His tactic entailed dividing his forces into three units to encircle the Lunga area from the land, climaxing in a nocturnal surprise onslaught. Oka's troops would target the perimeter from the west, whereas the rebranded Ichiki's Second Echelon, now the Kuma Battalion, would come from the east. Kawaguchi's principal force, termed the "Center Body" and consisting of three battalions with 3,000 soldiers, would initiate their assault from the dense forests lying south of the Lunga defenses. By the day's end, a significant portion of Kawaguchi's forces had left Taivu, commencing their trek along the shoreline towards Lunga Point. However, a contingent of about 250 Japanese soldiers stayed back to oversee the brigade's resource base at Taivu.

In parallel, indigenous scouts, directed by Martin Clemens, an officer in the British Solomon Islands Protectorate Defence Force and the region's British representative, relayed intelligence to the U.S. Marines about Japanese troops stationed near Tasimboko village at Taivu. Recognizing an opportunity, Edson orchestrated a strike on this Japanese assembly at Taivu. The subsequent day, upon reaching near Taivu via boats, Edson and his forces overtook Tasimboko, with the Japanese opposition retreating into the wilderness. Within Tasimboko, they stumbled upon Kawaguchi's pivotal supply center, replete with substantial reserves of provisions, ammunition, medical essentials, and a potent shortwave radio. They demolished the found resources, retaining some documents and equipment. The discovered supplies and intelligence from the secured documents signaled to the Marines about the presence of around 3,000 Japanese soldiers on Guadalcanal, evidently scheming an offensive.

Both Edson and Colonel Gerald C. Thomas, an aide to Vandegrift, accurately anticipated the Japanese offensive targeting the Lunga Ridge. This slim, grass-covered, 1,000-yard-long coral ridge, running adjacent to the Lunga River and situated just to Henderson Field's south, presented a logical path to the airstrip, dominated its surroundings, and was barely defended. By the 11th of September, Edson's battalion, comprising 840 personnel, took positions across this ridge.

On the evening of 12 September, the 1st Battalion under Kawaguchi clashed with the Raiders between the Lunga River and the ridge. This forced a Marine company to retreat to the ridge's safety before the Japanese paused their offensive for the night. The subsequent evening saw Kawaguchi's brigade, 3,000-strong and accompanied by light artillery, challenging Edson's 840 Raiders. As darkness fell, Kawaguchi's 1st battalion initiated an assault on Edson's right flank, situated just west of the ridge. Despite initial breakthroughs in the Marine defenses, they were eventually halted by Marine contingents defending the ridge's northern segment.

Meanwhile, two companies from Kawaguchi's 2nd Battalion escalated their assault on the ridge's southern tip, pushing the Raiders back towards Hill 123, located centrally on the ridge. Throughout the nighttime, Marines stationed here withstood relentless Japanese offensives, backed by artillery. Some confrontations descended into brutal close-quarters combat. Japanese factions that maneuvered past the ridge towards the airstrip's vicinity were also driven back. Concurrent assaults by the Kuma Battalion and Oka's group at different points along the Lunga defenses met with similar fates. By 14 September, Kawaguchi, leading what remained of his beleaguered brigade, embarked on a five-day trek westward to the Matanikau Valley, intending to regroup with Oka's detachment. Kawaguchi's units suffered a loss of approximately 850 soldiers, while the Marines counted 104 casualties.

On 15 September, upon hearing of Kawaguchi's setback at Rabaul, Hyakutake relayed the update to the Imperial General Headquarters in Japan. In an urgent meeting, the highest echelons of the Japanese IJA and IJN deduced that "Guadalcanal could be the pivotal battle of the war." This conflict's outcome began influencing Japanese strategies across the Pacific. Hyakutake acknowledged the dilemma of allocating enough resources and troops to both counter the Allies on Guadalcanal and sustain the significant Japanese push on the Kokoda Track in New Guinea. Thus, with the approval of the General Headquarters, he directed his forces in New Guinea, who were a mere 30 miles away from their target, Port Moresby, to retreat and prioritize the "Guadalcanal situation." Hyakutake then commenced arrangements to deploy additional troops to Guadalcanal, aiming to reclaim Henderson Field.

As the U.S. fortified their Lunga defenses, the Japanese regrouped to the west of Matanikau. On September 14, Vandegrift transferred the 3rd Battalion of the 2nd Marine Regiment from Tulagi to Guadalcanal. A few days later, on September 18, an Allied naval convoy landed 4,157 troops from the 3rd Provisional Marine Brigade, which included the 7th Marine Regiment, a battalion from the 11th Marine Regiment, and other supporting units. Additionally, 137 vehicles, tents, aviation fuel, rations, ammunition, and other critical supplies were offloaded. With these reinforcements at his disposal, Vandegrift began establishing a continuous defense line around the Lunga perimeter on September 19.

However, during the protection of this convoy, the aircraft carrier USS Wasp was critically damaged by torpedoes from Japanese submarine I-19 and subsequently scuttled southeast of Guadalcanal. This incident left the Allies with only one operational aircraft carrier, the USS Hornet, in the South Pacific.

Vandegrift also evaluated and adjusted his leadership. He relieved certain senior officers who didn't meet his expectations and promoted capable junior officers to replace them. Notably, Colonel Merritt Edson was promoted and given command of the 5th Marine Regiment.

A brief hiatus in the aerial combat ensued from September 14-27, due to unfavorable weather. This pause allowed both sides to bolster their aerial units. The Japanese dispatched 85 aircraft to Rabaul, while the U.S. added 23 to Henderson Field. By September 20, the Japanese had 117 aircraft stationed at Rabaul, and the Allies had 71 at Henderson Field. The aerial confrontations recommenced on September 27 when Japanese aircraft engaged U.S. Navy and Marine fighters from Henderson Field.

Subsequent to their previous setback, the Japanese commenced preparations to retake Henderson Field. The 3rd Battalion of the 4th (Aoba) Infantry Regiment, which had arrived at Kamimbo Bay on Guadalcanal's western edge on September 11, now aligned with Oka's units near the Matanikau. Tokyo Express missions on September 14, 20, 21, and 24 supplied ammunition, food, and 280 soldiers from the 1st Battalion, Aoba Regiment, to Kamimbo Bay. Concurrently, the Japanese began transporting the 2nd and 38th Infantry Divisions from the Dutch East Indies to Rabaul from September 13. Their strategy involved dispatching 17,500 soldiers from these divisions to Guadalcanal, aiming for a large-scale assault on the Lunga perimeter by the end of October.

Vandegrift and his team recognized that Kawaguchi's forces had retreated westward of the Matanikau, with several Japanese groups dispersed between the Lunga perimeter and the Matanikau River. Consequently, Vandegrift initiated a sequence of operations around the Matanikau Valley. These tactics aimed to clear out the isolated Japanese units east of the Matanikau and disrupt the main Japanese force, preventing them from establishing their foothold too close to the primary Marine defenses at Lunga Point.

From September 23 to 27, U.S. Marine units launched an operation targeting Japanese positions west of the Matanikau. However, the Marine attack met stiff resistance from Kawaguchi's forces, now under the direct leadership of Akinosuke Oka. During the ensuing battle, three Marine companies found themselves encircled near Point Cruz, west of the Matanikau. Facing heavy casualties, they narrowly managed an escape with the aid of the destroyer USS Monssen and landing crafts steered by U.S. Coast Guard members. Among them was Douglas Munro, who heroically used his vessel to shield the retreating Marines. In the process, Munro lost his life and posthumously received the Medal of Honor, becoming the only Coast Guardsman to earn this distinction.

In early October, a larger Marine detachment successfully traversed the Matanikau River and engaged newly-arrived Japanese troops from the 2nd Infantry Division, led by Generals Masao Maruyama and Yumio Nasu. The Marines inflicted significant casualties on the Japanese 4th Infantry Regiment, pushing them to withdraw from their eastern Matanikau positions. This setback disrupted the Japanese's strategic plans for a significant offensive against the U.S. defenses in Lunga. From October 9 to 11, the U.S. 1st Battalion 2nd Marines executed raids on two minor Japanese stations, approximately 30 miles east of the Lunga defensive line, near Aola Bay. These assaults resulted in the deaths of 35 Japanese soldiers, while the U.S. suffered a loss of 17 Marines and 3 Navy members.

During the closing days of September and early October, the Tokyo Express consistently ferried troops from Japan's 2nd Infantry Division to Guadalcanal. The Japanese Navy pledged to facilitate the Army's forthcoming offensive by ensuring the successful transport of troops, gear, and supplies to the island, amplifying air strikes on Henderson Field, and dispatching naval vessels to shell the airfield.

At this juncture, Millard F. Harmon, the head of U.S. Army forces in the South Pacific, persuaded Ghormley of the pressing need to augment U.S. Marine forces on Guadalcanal. This reinforcement was deemed crucial to fend off the anticipated Japanese assault. Consequently, on 8 October, the 2,837-strong 164th Infantry Regiment of the Americal Division embarked on ships in New Caledonia, setting sail for Guadalcanal with an expected arrival on 13 October. To shield these transport vessels, Ghormley directed Task Force 64, a fleet comprising four cruisers and five destroyers under Rear Admiral Norman Scott, to counter any Japanese naval threats.

For the night of 11 October, Mikawa's 8th Fleet orchestrated a pivotal Tokyo Express mission. The aim was to transport 728 soldiers, artillery, and ammunition to Guadalcanal with two seaplane carriers and six destroyers. Simultaneously, under Rear Admiral Aritomo Gotō's command, a separate unit consisting of three heavy cruisers and two destroyers was tasked to shell Henderson Field. As U.S. Navy vessels hadn't interfered with Tokyo Express missions previously, the Japanese weren't anticipating any naval confrontations that evening.

However, just before midnight, Admiral Scott's ships identified Gotō's contingent via radar. Positioned advantageously, Scott's fleet was ready to "cross the T" on Gotō's unprepared squadron. A fierce exchange ensued, resulting in Scott's forces sinking a cruiser and a destroyer and inflicting heavy damages on another cruiser. Gotō was fatally injured, prompting his remaining ships to retreat. Although Scott lost a destroyer and had two ships heavily damaged, the Japanese supply convoy managed to unload its cargo without being detected.

The following morning, four Japanese destroyers aimed to support Gotō's wounded fleet. However, aerial assaults from the CAF stationed at Henderson Field sank two of these destroyers later in the day. The U.S. Army's convoy reached Guadalcanal on 13 October, offloading its troops and supplies without incident.

Even after the U.S. triumph at Cape Esperance, Japan pressed ahead with their ambitious offensive set for later in October. In an unusual move, the Japanese opted for a strategy different from their norm of using only swift warships for their deliveries to the island. On 13 October, a flotilla consisting of six cargo vessels escorted by eight destroyers set sail from the Shortland Islands, bound for Guadalcanal. This fleet transported 4,500 soldiers from the 16th and 230th Infantry Regiments, alongside some naval marines, two artillery batteries, and a company of tanks.

To shield this convoy from potential CAF aircraft assaults, Yamamoto dispatched the 3rd Battleship Division, led by Takeo Kurita, from Truk, aiming to decimate Henderson Field. At 01:33 on 14 October, battleships Kongō and Haruna, accompanied by a light cruiser and nine destroyers, reached their target and unleashed a barrage on Henderson Field from around 16,000 meters away. Over the ensuing 83 minutes, they launched 973 14-inch shells predominantly onto the airfield, causing significant damage. This intense onslaught obliterated both runways, consumed nearly all the aviation fuel, destroyed 48 CAF aircraft, and resulted in 41 casualties, including six CAF pilots. The battleship group then promptly retreated to Truk.

Remarkably, the runway damage was partially mended within hours. Seventeen SBD-3 Dauntless dive bombers and 20 F4F Wildcats from Espiritu Santo were rapidly deployed to reinforce Henderson. Additionally, U.S. Army and Marine transport planes transferred aviation fuel from Espiritu Santo to Guadalcanal. Recognizing the impending arrival of the substantial Japanese convoy, the U.S. frantically sought means to intercept it. Despite their resourcefulness, using fuel from wrecked planes and a nearby stash, the CAF's two assaults on the convoy on 14 October proved futile.

On midnight of 14 October, the Japanese convoy anchored at Tassafaronga Point and started unloading. Throughout 15 October, a relentless barrage from CAF aircraft assailed the unloading convoy, sinking three cargo vessels. Nevertheless, by nightfall, the convoy had offloaded all the troops and approximately two-thirds of their provisions and gear. In addition, several Japanese cruisers shelled Henderson Field on the nights of 14 and 15 October. While they managed to destroy a few more CAF planes, they couldn't inflict substantial damage on the airfield.

From 1 to 17 October, the Japanese managed to deploy 15,000 soldiers to Guadalcanal, equipping Hyakutake with a total force of 20,000 for his upcoming offensive. Due to their setbacks on the east side of the Matanikau, they assessed that a coastal assault on the U.S. defenses would be overly challenging. As a result, Hyakutake strategized to launch the main offensive from the south of Henderson Field. Maruyama, leading the 2nd Division (strengthened by units from the 38th Division) which consisted of 7,000 troops spread across three regiments, was directed to navigate through the jungle and strike the American lines from the south, close to the Lunga River's eastern bank. Initially scheduled for 22 October, the assault was rescheduled to 23 October. To divert the Americans from this southern assault, Hyakutake tasked Major General Tadashi Sumiyoshi and his heavy artillery, supported by five battalions of infantry (roughly 2,900 troops), to challenge the U.S. defenses from the west along the coastal path. The Japanese, mistakenly believing they were up against 10,000 Americans, were actually facing a force of around 23,000.

On 12 October, Japanese engineers initiated the creation of a pathway, named the "Maruyama Road", starting from the Matanikau and leading towards the U.S. Lunga perimeter's southern region. This 15-mile trail was a challenging route that included various obstacles like multiple rivers and streams, deep and muddy trenches, steep ridges, and thick jungles. From 16 to 18 October, the 2nd Division embarked on their journey through this challenging path.

As of 23 October, Maruyama's troops were still navigating the dense jungle, attempting to approach the American defenses. In light of his troops' delay in reaching their designated positions, Hyakutake decided to reschedule the assault to 19:00 on 24 October. Meanwhile, the American forces remained oblivious to Maruyama's advancing troops.

Hyakutake's staff relayed the decision to delay the offensive to 24 October to Sumiyoshi, but he couldn't communicate this change in time to his frontline units. As a result, on the evening of 23 October, two battalions from the 4th Infantry Regiment, along with nine tanks from the 1st Independent Tank Company, commenced their assault on the U.S. Marine defenses near the Matanikau. Facing intense U.S. artillery, cannon, and gunfire, these attacks were thwarted, resulting in the destruction of all the tanks and significant Japanese casualties, while U.S. forces suffered minimal losses.

Late on 24 October, Maruyama's troops finally reached their intended attack position at the Lunga perimeter. Over the next two nights, they launched repeated frontal assaults against the U.S. defenses manned by the 1st Battalion, 7th Marines led by Lieutenant Colonel Chesty Puller and the 3rd Battalion, 164th Infantry Regiment under Lieutenant Colonel Robert Hall. These American forces, armed with a mix of rifles, machine guns, mortars, and artillery, inflicted significant damage on the Japanese attackers. Although a few Japanese units breached the U.S. lines, they were swiftly neutralized in subsequent operations. The assaults led to the deaths of over 1,500 Japanese soldiers, compared to around 60 American fatalities. Concurrently, American aircraft from Henderson Field countered Japanese air and naval forces, downing 14 aircraft and sinking a cruiser.

Subsequent Japanese offensives near the Matanikau on 26 October faced a similar fate. By the morning of that day, recognizing the futility of further assaults, Hyakutake ordered a retreat. Maruyama's remaining forces were divided, with some retreating to the Matanikau Valley and others, under Colonel Toshinari Shōji, heading east towards Koli Point. By 4 November, elements of the 2nd Division had reached the 17th Army's base at Kokumbona, while Shōji's contingent established their camp at Koli Point. Depleted from combat, injuries, malnutrition, and diseases, the 2nd Division transitioned to a defensive role for the remainder of the campaign. Overall, the battle resulted in the deaths of between 2,200 and 3,000 Japanese soldiers, while American casualties numbered approximately 80.

While Hyakutake's forces engaged on the Lunga perimeter, Japanese naval assets, including aircraft carriers directed by Yamamoto, positioned themselves near the southern Solomon Islands. Their objective was to decisively counter any Allied, primarily U.S., naval interventions in response to Hyakutake's ground movements. Conversely, the Allied naval forces in the region, under the leadership of William Halsey Jr., were eager to engage with their Japanese counterparts. On 18 October, Nimitz had replaced Ghormley with Admiral Halsey, believing that Ghormley had grown overly cautious and lacked the vision to effectively lead the Allied forces in the South Pacific Area.

The stage was set for a naval showdown on the morning of 26 October, culminating in the Battle of the Santa Cruz Islands. Following a series of air strikes from carriers on both sides, the Allied naval contingent had to withdraw, suffering the loss of one carrier, the Hornet, and significant damage to another, the Enterprise. In contrast, the Japanese carrier group, despite having the upper hand in ship damage dealt, chose to retreat due to the substantial loss of aircraft and experienced aircrews, as well as significant damage to two of their carriers. Even though the Japanese seemed to have achieved a tactical victory based on ship damage, the heavy loss of their seasoned aircrews tipped the strategic balance in favor of the Allies, who sustained comparatively minor aircrew casualties. Consequently, Japanese carriers had a diminished impact in the subsequent stages of the campaign.

Seeking to capitalize on their triumph in the Battle for Henderson Field, Vandegrift mobilized six Marine battalions, reinforced later by an Army battalion, for an assault west of the Matanikau. Merritt Edson led this operation, with the objective of seizing Kokumbona, the 17th Army's headquarters situated west of Point Cruz. Japanese defenses in this area, manned by the beleaguered 4th Infantry Regiment under Nomasu Nakaguma, were severely compromised due to combat losses, illnesses, and malnutrition.

Initiating their assault on 1 November, the American forces overcame the Japanese defenses around Point Cruz by 3 November, neutralizing reinforcements dispatched to bolster Nakaguma's dwindling regiment. Just when the Americans seemed poised to capture Kokumbona, they stumbled upon fresh Japanese forces near Koli Point to the east of the Lunga perimeter. As a result, Vandegrift halted the Matanikau assault on 4 November. Casualties from the American side stood at 71, while the Japanese lost around 400 soldiers.

At dawn on 3 November, five Japanese destroyers offloaded 300 troops at Koli Point, intended to bolster Shōji's units moving towards the area after their engagement at Henderson Field. Forewarned about this maneuver, Vandegrift dispatched a Marine battalion led by Herman H. Hanneken to intercept them. However, the Japanese forces managed to push Hanneken's battalion back. In retaliation, Vandegrift sent additional troops, including Puller's Marine battalion and two battalions from the 164th infantry, to counter the Japanese at Koli Point.

With American troops closing in and Hyakutake instructing Shōji to regroup with the Japanese at Kokumbona, Shōji and 2,000 to 3,000 of his soldiers managed to escape via a marshy creek on the American flank between 9 and 11 November. By 12 November, the remaining Japanese soldiers at Koli Point were overrun. In the aftermath, Americans tallied 450–475 Japanese casualties, capturing most of Shōji's equipment and supplies. The operation resulted in 40 American deaths and 120 wounded.

Concurrently, on 4 November, units from the 2nd Marine Raider Battalion, led by Lieutenant Colonel Evans Carlson, landed at Aola Bay, 40 miles east of Lunga Point. Their task was to guard 500 Seabees constructing an airfield, an endeavor that was ultimately abandoned by month's end due to unsuitable terrain.

On 5 November, Carlson and his raiders were directed to intercept any remnants of Shōji's troops retreating from Koli Point. Over a span of 29 days, Carlson's unit engaged Shōji's retreating soldiers multiple times, inflicting nearly 500 casualties while losing 16 of their own. Tropical diseases and a food shortage further decimated Shōji's troops. By mid-November, as they approached the Lunga River, only a fraction remained, and upon reaching the 17th Army positions, merely 700 to 800 soldiers were left. The survivors then bolstered Japanese defenses in the Mount Austen and upper Matanikau River areas.

Further troop deployments by the Tokyo Express between 5 and 9 November strengthened Japanese positions in the Point Cruz and Matanikau areas, allowing them to fend off American assaults on 10 and 18 November. Both armies remained in a standoff near Point Cruz for the subsequent six weeks.

The Battle for Henderson Field was a pivotal engagement during World War II. After their setback, the Imperial Japanese Army (IJA) strategized another attempt to reclaim the airfield in November 1942. However, they required additional forces for this endeavor. Assistance was sought from Yamamoto, who dispatched 11 transport ships carrying 7,000 soldiers from the 38th Infantry Division, along with their supplies and equipment, from Rabaul to Guadalcanal. He also dispatched a fleet led by the battleships Hiei and Kirishima, tasked with neutralizing Henderson Field on the night of 12-13 November to ease the transport ships' landing.

By early November, Allies caught wind of the Japanese plan to retake the field. In reaction, the U.S. deployed Task Force 67, equipped with Marine reinforcements, U.S. Army infantry, and supplies, to Guadalcanal on 11

November. This convoy, overseen by Turner, was protected by fleets under Rear Admirals Callaghan and Scott, and aircraft from the coveted Henderson Field. Despite being targeted by Japanese aircraft on 11 and 12 November, most of these ships were safely unloaded.

U.S. aircraft soon detected the nearing Japanese bombardment fleet and relayed this to Allied leadership. Consequently, Turner instructed all combat-ready ships under Callaghan to shield the troops onshore and signaled the supply vessels to leave by the evening of 12 November. Callaghan's fleet encountered Abe's fleet near Guadalcanal in the early hours of 13 November. A fierce battle ensued, leading to significant damage to both sides. Notably, both Callaghan and Scott perished in the confrontation. Though Abe's forces had the upper hand, he decided to retreat without bombarding Henderson Field. The damaged Hiei later sank due to sustained aerial assaults. Yamamoto, responding to Abe's decision, postponed the troop transport convoy's advance towards Guadalcanal.

In the subsequent days, another Japanese fleet bombarded Henderson Field, causing limited damage. Assuming the field was compromised, Tanaka's transport convoy advanced towards Guadalcanal. However, relentless attacks from Henderson Field and the aircraft carrier Enterprise decimated the convoy. Simultaneously, Kondō's fleet approached for another bombardment.

Anticipating Kondō's move, Halsey dispatched a U.S. fleet, including the battleships Washington and South Dakota. These forces clashed on the night of 14 November. The U.S. lost three destroyers, but the Washington managed to cripple the Kirishima. With his forces reeling, Kondō withdrew, again leaving Henderson Field unscathed.

As Kondō's fleet withdrew, the four Japanese transport vessels found themselves stranded near Tassafaronga Point on Guadalcanal around 04:00. By 05:55, these beached vessels came under a barrage from U.S. aircraft and artillery. This assault resulted in the destruction of all four ships, along with a majority of their cargo. Only a fraction, about 2,000–3,000 soldiers, managed to disembark. Given the unsuccessful reinforcement and supply efforts, the Japanese had no choice but to call off their intended November assault on Henderson Field. This marked a crucial strategic win for the Allies and signified a downturn in Japanese endeavors to reclaim the coveted airfield.

On 26 November, the leadership saw a change with Lieutenant General Hitoshi Imamura assuming control of the freshly instituted Eighth Area Army at Rabaul. This new authority spanned both the 17th Army under Hyakutake and the 18th Army in New Guinea. One of Imamura's initial objectives was to persist in the effort to reclaim Henderson Field and the broader Guadalcanal. However, the situation shifted when the Allies launched an offensive at Buna in New Guinea. Viewing this new offensive as a direct threat to Rabaul, Imamura decided to redirect his focus and resources to New Guinea, leaving Guadalcanal as a secondary concern.

The Japanese faced persistent challenges in getting adequate supplies to their troops on Guadalcanal. Relying solely on submarines for the last half of November proved insufficient in meeting the demands of Hyakutake's troops. Efforts to establish bases in the central Solomons to ease barge supply routes to Guadalcanal were thwarted by relentless Allied aerial offensives. By 26 November, the 17th Army relayed to Imamura a looming food shortage. Some units hadn't received supplies in nearly a week, prompting the Japanese to revert to using destroyers for essential deliveries.

In an inventive bid to minimize the vulnerability of these destroyers, the Eighth Fleet developed a new delivery technique. They cleaned large fuel drums, filled them with essentials, ensuring they had enough air to float, and tied them together. As destroyers neared Guadalcanal, a swift turn would release the drums. Swimmers or boats from the shore could then retrieve these supplies.

On the night of 30 November, Tanaka, leading the Guadalcanal Reinforcement

Unit of the Eighth Fleet, attempted the drum delivery method using eight destroyers. Aware of this plan, Halsey directed Task Force 67, consisting of four cruisers and four destroyers under Rear Admiral Carleton H. Wright, to intercept them.

By 22:40, as Tanaka's ships reached Guadalcanal, Wright's fleet approached from the opposite direction. Wright's ships, detecting the Japanese on radar, sought permission to unleash their torpedoes. A delay in approval meant a missed opportunity, with all U.S. torpedoes failing to hit their mark. In retaliation, Tanaka's fleet released 44 torpedoes towards Wright's cruisers, causing significant damage and sinking the U.S. cruiser Northampton. Tanaka's remaining destroyers retreated unharmed but didn't deliver the supplies.

By 7 December, the dire supply situation worsened, with Hyakutake's troops facing significant daily casualties due to lack of nutrition, illness, and Allied attacks. Further delivery attempts in December by Tanaka were largely unsuccessful, with one destroyer even being sunk by a U.S. PT boat.

On 12 December, the Japanese Naval leadership suggested the possibility of abandoning Guadalcanal. Simultaneously, some staff officers from the Imperial General Headquarters (IGH) also expressed doubts about recapturing Guadalcanal. Later that month, a team led by Colonel Joichiro Sanada, the head of the IGH operations section, traveled to Rabaul to meet with Imamura and his officers. After their consultations, Sanada returned to Tokyo and advised that Guadalcanal should be given up. By 26 December, the top brass at IGH concurred with Sanada's assessment and initiated plans for a retreat from Guadalcanal, intending to set up a new defensive line in the central Solomons while redirecting efforts and resources to New Guinea.

On 28 December, Emperor Hirohito was briefed about the decision to pull out from Guadalcanal by General Hajime Sugiyama and Admiral Osami Nagano. Three days later, the Emperor officially approved the withdrawal.

Subsequently, the Japanese covertly began laying the groundwork for the evacuation, code-named Operation Ke, slated to commence in late January 1943.

In December, the fatigued 1st Marine Division was relieved for rest and recovery, and the U.S. XIV Corps took charge of the island's operations in the subsequent month. The corps was made up of the 2nd Marine Division and the 25th Infantry and 23rd bDivisions from the U.S. Army. Command of the Allied forces on Guadalcanal transitioned to U.S. Army Major General Alexander Patch from Vandegrift. By January, the Allied forces numbered slightly over 50,000 personnel.

On 18 December, the Allies, primarily U.S. Army troops, launched an assault on Japanese positions at Mount Austen. However, the fortified Japanese position known as the Gifu proved a tough challenge, causing the Allies to pause their offensive by 4 January. The assault resumed on 10 January, targeting Japanese defenses on Mount Austen and the adjacent ridges known as the Sea Horse and Galloping Horse. By 23 January, after facing intense resistance, the Allies secured all three positions. Concurrently, U.S. Marines made significant advancements along the island's northern coastline. Throughout this operation, the Americans incurred approximately 250 casualties, whereas the Japanese had close to 3,000 losses, marking a 12 to 1 ratio in favor of the Americans.

On 14 January, a Tokyo Express mission brought in a battalion meant to safeguard the rear during the Ke evacuation. Along with them, a staff officer from Rabaul arrived to inform Hyakutake of the impending withdrawal. Concurrently, Japanese military assets, both aerial and naval, were positioned around Rabaul and Bougainville, gearing up for the pullout. Allied analysts noticed these movements but mistakenly thought they indicated a renewed effort to reclaim Henderson Field and Guadalcanal.

In response to this perceived threat, Patch, being cautious, deployed only a small fraction of his forces to steadily push against Hyakutake's defenses. On 29 January, based on the same flawed intelligence, Halsey dispatched a supply convoy to Guadalcanal, protected by a group of cruisers. Upon spotting these cruisers, Japanese torpedo bombers initiated an assault, inflicting heavy damage on the cruiser Chicago. The subsequent day saw another wave of torpedo bombers, which resulted in the sinking of Chicago. In the aftermath, Halsey called back the residual task force and repositioned his naval units in the Coral Sea, south of Guadalcanal, to brace for the anticipated Japanese onslaught.

Simultaneously, the Japanese 17th Army started its retreat to Guadalcanal's western coast, while units forming the rear guard kept the American advance at bay. On the evening of 1 February, a fleet of 20 destroyers led by Shintarō Hashimoto of Mikawa's 8th Fleet successfully evacuated 4,935 troops, primarily from the 38th Division. Both the Japanese and the Americans lost a destroyer during the evacuation-related air and naval confrontations.

Over the nights of 4 and 7 February, Hashimoto and his fleet managed to pull out the rest of the Japanese forces from Guadalcanal. With only a few aerial skirmishes, the Allies, still expecting a significant Japanese strike, didn't interfere with the evacuations. In the end, the Japanese managed to extract 10,652 personnel from Guadalcanal. Their final departure took place on the evening of 7 February, marking exactly six months since the initial U.S. landing. By 9 February, Patch recognized the Japanese absence and proclaimed Guadalcanal to be secured.

Following the retreat of the Japanese, Guadalcanal and Tulagi became pivotal bases facilitating the Allies' progress up the Solomon Islands. In addition to Henderson Field, two more runways for fighters were established at Lunga Point, while a bomber airfield was set up at Koli Point. Comprehensive naval and logistical facilities were created at Guadalcanal, Tulagi, and Florida. The Tulagi anchorage evolved into a significant forward hub for Allied naval and transport vessels, aiding the Solomon Islands campaign. Before being deployed up the Solomons, major ground units utilized vast camps and quarters on Guadalcanal for staging.

Post-Guadalcanal, the tide clearly turned against the Japanese in the Pacific. Their continual need to bolster Guadalcanal diluted their strengths across other fronts, paving the way for a triumphant Australian and American counter-push in New Guinea. This led to the seizure of essential bases like Buna and Gona by early 1943. The Allies had clinched a strategic upper hand that they maintained throughout. In June, the Allies initiated Operation Cartwheel. Its subsequent revision in August 1943 underscored the strategy to corner Rabaul and sever its maritime supply routes. The ensuing effective neutralization of Rabaul and its forces enabled the South West Pacific campaign spearheaded by MacArthur and the Central Pacific island-hopping strategy led by Nimitz. Both campaigns progressively advanced towards Japan, with the remaining Japanese defenses in the South Pacific being either vanquished or circumvented by Allied troops as the war unfolded.

The Battle of Milne Bay

I n early December 1941, the Japanese initiated their Pacific campaign, targeting British and Commonwealth forces in the Battle of Hong Kong and the Malayan campaign, while also launching a surprise attack on the US Pacific Fleet at Pearl Harbor. Quickly progressing southward, they overran resistance in Malaya, seized Singapore by February 1942, and effectively occupied Timor, Rabaul, and the Dutch East Indies. Despite their setback in the Battle of the Coral Sea in May, they made significant gains elsewhere, notably conquering the Philippines and pushing towards India through Burma.

Even though the Japanese faced defeat in the Coral Sea, the Allies anticipated another attempt to capture Port Moresby. To safeguard this critical location, General Douglas MacArthur, the Supreme Commander of the South West Pacific Area, sought to establish airbases in its vicinity. He sanctioned the construction of one airbase at Merauke in Netherlands New Guinea to the west, and proposed another, "Boston," to the east in the Abau–Mullins Harbour area on 20 May. These bases would strategically sit on the path any Japanese naval force would take to reach Port Moresby, enabling early detection and confrontation. Additionally, the eastern base would enable bombers to strike Rabaul and other northern Japanese strongholds without navigating the treacherous Owen Stanley Range. Consequently, an airstrip apt for heavy bombers was envisioned to link with Port Moresby and northern Australian bases.

On 24 May, General Sir Thomas Blamey, Chief of Allied Land Forces, designated a Boston garrison. However, the troops were strictly instructed to fend off only minor Japanese incursions, retreating and destroying valuable assets in the face of a significant assault. Plans for Boston were later abandoned due to unfavorable site assessments, with Milne Bay emerging as a preferable alternative. A joint team of Americans and Australians scouted Milne Bay on 8 June, praising its terrain, road infrastructure, and jetties, all favorable for airbase establishment. Following their positive report, MacArthur's General Headquarters (GHQ) swapped the Boston project for Milne Bay on 11 June, naming it "Fall River". However, using geographic names as codenames led to logistical hiccups, with some supplies mistakenly shipped to the actual Fall River in Massachusetts.

Troops first set foot at Milne Bay on 25 June, transported from Port Moresby aboard the Dutch KPM vessels Karsik and Bontekoe. The ships were accompanied by HMAS Warrego and HMAS Ballarat. The Karsik anchored at an improvised pontoon wharf, hastily assembled by Papuan workers under the guidance of ANGAU, who then assisted in unloading the vessels. Among the troops were segments from the 55th Infantry Battalion, the 9th Light Anti-Aircraft Battery, a platoon from the US 101st Coast Artillery Battalion, and two anti-aircraft guns from the 23rd Heavy Anti-Aircraft Battery. Additionally, Company E from the US Army Corps of Engineers' 46th Engineers, equipped for airbase construction, disembarked from the Bontekoe. It's noteworthy that, post the fall of the Dutch East Indies, 29 KPM ships fled to Australia. These ships, manned by Dutch and Javanese crews, significantly bolstered the Milne Bay garrison. Unfortunately, five KPM vessels were later lost amidst the Papua conflicts.

By 8 June, work had already started on the first airfield, later named No. 1 Airstrip. Papuan workers, overseen by ANGAU, along with personnel from the US 96th Engineer Separate Battalion, commenced the clearance near Gili Gili. Company E of the 46th Engineers began their operations on the airstrip on 30 June. Their tasks encompassed the construction of the runway, camouflaged dispersal areas for 32 fighter planes, taxiways, and accommodation facilities for 500 personnel. Moreover, a platoon was reassigned to enhance the docks and roadways. Though Milne Bay's channels allowed larger ships to approach the shore closely, unloading supplies required pontoons and manual labor, making the task quite demanding.

On 22 July, the airstrip witnessed the landing of three Kittyhawks from No. 76 Squadron RAAF. Additional aircraft from both No. 76 and No. 75 Squadron RAAF touched down on 25 July. The pilots noted that the 6,000-by-100-foot airstrip was partially covered with Marston Matting, with frequent waterlogging. Consequently, landing planes would disperse water, occasionally veering off the runway and getting stuck in the mud.

With No. 1 Airstrip in operation, efforts shifted to constructing two additional airfields. No. 2 Airstrip saw the removal of approximately 5,000 coconut trees. However, before its utilization, two bridges measuring at least 60 feet each needed construction. Therefore, focus redirected to No. 3 Airstrip near Kilarbo. The 2nd Battalion of the US 43rd Engineers, excluding Company E, took on this task, arriving on 4 August. That very day, Japanese planes targeted Milne Bay, primarily aiming at the airstrips and engineers. One Kittyhawk was destroyed, but another from No. 76 Squadron managed to down a dive bomber. To counter this threat, the Australians set up a radar system for advanced warnings. A skirmish on 11 August saw 22 Kittyhawks facing 12 Zeroes. Despite outnumbering the enemy, three Australian Kittyhawks were lost, with four Japanese Zeros claimed downed.

On 11 July, the 7th Infantry Brigade, led by Brigadier John Field, started pouring into the area. This brigade had three Queensland Militia battalions: the 9th, 25th, and 61st Infantry Battalions. Additionally, they were equipped with guns from various artillery units and the first Australian engineer unit, the 24th Field Company. Field took charge of "Milne Force", overseeing all Allied operations in the vicinity and directly liaising with Blamey's Allied Land Forces in Brisbane. A significant portion of his immediate responsibilities involved engineering tasks. While the American engineers focused on the airstrips and docks, Australian units worked on infrastructure and accommodation, often supplemented by infantry and local Papuan workers.

Malaria was a known concern in the Milne Bay region, yet precautions against it were inconsistent. Soldiers wore short clothing, relied on ineffective mosquito repellents, and many lacked mosquito nets due to logistics issues. Additionally, there was a shortage of quinine, a crucial anti-malarial drug. Many soldiers, advised to delay quinine consumption until after their first week, contracted the disease by then. Brigadier Neil Hamilton Fairley, an expert in tropical medicine, recognized the severe threat malaria posed to the Allied forces in Papua. While he ensured ample medical provisions were dispatched to Milne Bay, including quinine tablets, some supplies got damaged or lost in transit. The gravity of the malaria threat wasn't fully grasped at Milne Bay at this stage.

By early August, companies from the 55th Infantry Battalion, weakened by malaria and other tropical ailments, were repositioned to Port Moresby. Nevertheless, the stronghold at Milne Bay was bolstered with the arrival of Brigadier George Wootten's 18th Infantry Brigade of the 7th Division on 12 August. This esteemed brigade, with prior combat experience from the siege of Tobruk, encompassed the 2/9th, 2/10th, and 2/12th Infantry Battalions. Their defensive efforts were augmented with anti-aircraft and artillery units, along with various logistical and communication troops.

Major General Cyril Clowes was designated as the leader of Milne Force on 12 August. He and his central team flew into Milne Bay. Despite his arrival on 13 August, Clowes had to wait for the remainder of his personnel before officially taking the reins of Milne Force on 22 August. By that period, Milne Bay was fortified with roughly 7,459 Australian and 1,365 US Army staff, with about 4,500 serving as infantry. An additional contingent of around 600 RAAF individuals was also present.

Clowes tasked the relatively green 7th Infantry Brigade with safeguarding crucial areas around Milne Bay against potential maritime or aerial offensives, while reserving the battle-hardened 18th Infantry Brigade for potential counter-strikes. Hindered by the absence of precise maps and unreliable communication gear under the existing conditions, the Australian command largely depended on wired telephones. In cases where adequate lines were unavailable, they resorted to dispatch runners. The marshy terrain further hampered vehicular and even pedestrian mobility.

The Allies' strategic positioning at Milne Bay didn't go unnoticed by Japanese aerial reconnaissance. Recognizing the significant threat it posed to their upcoming maritime push towards Port Moresby—set to initiate with a landing near Samarai Island, closely situated to Milne Bay—Lieutenant General Harukichi Hyakutake, leader of the Japanese XVII Army, urged the 8th Fleet under Vice Admiral Gunichi Mikawa to redirect its focus from Samarai to seizing the nascent Allied base at Milne Bay. Consequently, Mikawa revised the operation, which was now termed Operation RE and slated for mid-August. The urgency for this mission intensified after the 25th Air Flotilla identified the Milne Bay airstrips on 4 August. However, the operation was deferred due to American forces establishing their foothold on Guadalcanal on 7 August.

Believing that only two or three Australian infantry companies (300–600 men) were guarding the airfields, the initial Japanese assault force was comprised of around 1,250 personnel. The Imperial Japanese Army (IJA) was hesitant about the operation, fearing that Allied aircraft might attack any landing barges deployed to the region. After a disagreement between the IJA and the Imperial Japanese Navy (IJN), it was settled that the Navy would oversee the landing. Consequently, the attacking force came from the Japanese naval infantry, or Kaigun Rikusentai (Special Naval Landing Forces). Around 612 naval soldiers from the 5th Kure Special Naval Landing Force (SNLF), under Commander Masajiro Hayashi, were designated to land on the east coast near a location termed "Rabi" by the Japanese. They were accompanied by 197 men from the 5th Sasebo SNLF, headed by Lieutenant

Fujikawa. An additional 350 troops from the 10th Naval Landing Force and 100 from the 2nd Air Advance Party were set to land at Taupota, in Goodenough Bay, on the peninsula's northern coast. Their objective was to traverse the Stirling Ranges and ambush the Australians from the rear. Post-battle, Vice Admiral Matome Ugaki, the chief of staff of the Japanese Combined Fleet, observed that many in the landing force were 30- to 35-year-old soldiers lacking full fitness and optimal combat morale. Rear Admiral Mitsuharu Matsuyama's 18th Cruiser Division was tasked with providing naval support. The Japanese initially had an edge with their two Type-95 light tanks. But after their first assault, these tanks got stuck in the mud and were left behind. The Japanese maintained nocturnal sea control, facilitating reinforcement and evacuation operations.

In contrast to the Japanese's tactical strengths, the Allies held a significant strategic edge due to superior intelligence regarding Japanese intentions. While the Japanese had limited information about the Allied presence at Milne Bay, the Allies were forewarned about the impending Japanese invasion. In mid-July, codebreakers led by Commander Eric Nave briefed MacArthur about a projected Japanese assault on Milne Bay towards the end of August. They provided specifics such as the number of troops, the involved units, their training level, and the ships designated for the operation.

Brigadier General Charles A. Willoughby, MacArthur's Chief of Intelligence, had already anticipated a Japanese move against the Milne Force. He saw Japanese reconnaissance on August 4 as a precursor to a potential operation. Signals intelligence from the Allied Naval Forces, under the codename Ultra (which encompassed several codes, including the Japanese naval code JN-25), intercepted a message revealing a Japanese submarine line covering the Milne Bay approaches. This made Willoughby certain of an imminent attack.

Reacting to this intel, MacArthur quickly dispatched the 18th Infantry Brigade to Milne Bay. Major General George Kenney, head of the Allied Air Forces, increased air patrols over potential Japanese invasion paths. He also authorized pre-emptive strikes against the Japanese airfields at Buna on August 24 and 25, effectively reducing the available Japanese fighter support for the Milne Bay assault to a mere six aircraft.

On 23 and 24 August, planes from the 25th Air Flotilla executed preparatory bombings around Rabi's airfield. The primary Japanese invasion fleet, commanded by Matsuyama, departed Rabaul at 7:00 am on 24 August. This fleet included two light cruisers, Tenryū and Tatsuta, three destroyers, Urakaze, Tanikaze, and Hamakaze, as well as the transports Nankai Maru and Kinai Maru, with the submarine chasers CH-22 and CH-24.

By 8:30 am the next day, a Japanese convoy heading toward Milne Bay was sighted by an RAAF Hudson bomber near Kitava Island and by coastwatchers. HMAS Arunta, escorting the SS Tasman, departed Milne Bay for Port Moresby upon hearing about the invading force. Another Japanese convoy with seven barges from Buna, intended to land at Taupota, was also reported. Once the weather cleared, 12 RAAF Kittyhawks were dispatched. They found the barges on Goodenough Island's beach, where the 350 troops of the 5th Sasebo SNLF had disembarked to rest. The Australian pilots successfully destroyed all the barges, stranding the troops.

While the main invasion force evaded detection until 25 August, US B-17s tried to intercept but were deterred by inclement weather. Later, several Kittyhawks and a Hudson bomber launched an attack on the convoy near Rabi Island, causing minor damage. With the departure of HMAS Arunta and SS Tasman, the RAAF deployed a tender to scout the bay for early alerts of Japanese arrivals.

During this time, Clowes ordered a strategic repositioning. D Company of the 61st Infantry Battalion, previously at Akioma, was instructed to move behind 'B' Company at KB Mission and set up at the No. 3 Airstrip at Gili Gili. Their move, delayed due to a shortage of vessels, eventually utilized three luggers: Bronzewing, Elevala, and Dadosee. By 10:30 pm, over 1,000

Japanese troops, with two Type 95 Ha-Go tanks, had landed near Waga Waga, albeit off-course. They quickly began to secure their location, detaining local villagers and setting up a beachhead.

That night, D Company's withdrawal vessels encountered the Japanese landing party. A skirmish broke out, resulting in Elevala being beached. Its crew escaped into the jungle on foot, reaching Gili Gili later. Meanwhile, Bronzewing was damaged, and 11 of its occupants were either killed in the encounter or captured and subsequently executed by the Japanese.

On the morning of 26 August, the Japanese, with the aid of armor, advanced westward towards the coast, reaching the primary defense line held by B Company, 61st Infantry Battalion, near KB Mission. Leading their force through the jungle along the coastal path were two light tanks. Despite the Australians' lack of anti-tank weaponry, they managed to repel the Japanese assault. However, the situation worsened for the Japanese when their base was heavily bombed at dawn by a combined force of RAAF Kittyhawks, a Hudson aircraft, and US Fifth Air Force's B-25s, B-26s, and B-17s. This assault resulted in significant Japanese casualties, destruction of their supplies, and the loss of many beached landing barges near the KB Mission. The loss of these barges not only disrupted Japanese supplies but also halted any plans to outmaneuver the Australian battalions. Compounding their challenges, the Japanese lacked air cover; their fighters from Buna were swiftly downed by Allied aircraft, and other planes from Rabaul were forced to retreat due to adverse weather.

Despite these setbacks, the Japanese continued to pressure the positions held by the 61st Infantry Battalion. In response, Field, who oversaw the region, dispatched two platoons from the 25th Infantry Battalion for reinforcement. Additionally, the rest of the rifle companies from the 61st, along with their mortar platoon, were sent into action. The challenging muddy terrain prevented the Australians from positioning their anti-tank guns effectively. As a makeshift solution, they distributed sticky bombs and anti-tank mines to their front lines. By 4:45 pm, with the assistance of air and artillery, the Australians initiated a counter-attack on the Japanese's forward posts, located roughly 600 yards east of the mission, pushing them back around 200 yards. Exhausted from the day's combat, the Australians later retreated to Motieau, situated west of the mission.

As darkness loomed, the Australians tried to disengage and fall back towards a nearby creek, aiming to fortify a defensive position. Yet, the Japanese were relentless, continuously pressuring the retreating Australians. B Company rallied to fortify their new position, while the 2/10th Infantry Battalion prepared to move east through the 25th and 61st Infantry Battalions. That night, the Japanese ships targeted Australian defenses, and a subsequent heavy assault continued intermittently until the early hours. By dawn, the Japanese adopted covert tactics, aiming to bypass Australian defenses. Preempting a dawn armored strike, the Australians retreated to the Gama River.

As day broke, Japanese aircraft attacked the Allied Gili Gili airfield, inflicting minimal damage. Meanwhile, near the mission, the 2/10th Infantry Battalion, a unit of around 420 soldiers, was sent to the Gama River. Their mission was ambiguous, and the battalion ventured beyond the main defense lines without adequate intel or reinforcement prospects. Around 8:00 pm, the Japanese deployed tanks with glaring headlights. The 2/10th attempted to neutralize them using adhesive explosives, but humid conditions rendered them ineffective. Following a strenuous combat lasting two and a half hours, and with artillery backup from the 2/5th Field Regiment near Gili Gili, the Australians repelled multiple assaults. Nevertheless, by midnight, Japanese forces penetrated Australian lines, causing the 2/10th to fall back.

Subsequently, the 25th Infantry Battalion advanced from Gili Gili to relieve the 61st. They fortified positions around a still-under-construction airstrip, offering a clear line of sight and mud barriers preventing tank movements. Japanese forces, backed by artillery and tank support, initiated an attack at dawn. Unbeknownst to the Australians, the tanks were immobilized in mud. With support from the 25th, 61st Infantry Battalions, and American anti-aircraft troops, the Japanese infantry was repelled. Subsequent airstrikes forced the Japanese further back.

A two-day pause in hostilities followed. The Australians strengthened their defenses with the battered 61st Infantry Battalion returning to the perimeter around the airstrip. They collaborated with the 25th Battalion and received mortar and machine-gun support, with American engineers and anti-aircraft personnel participating in their first ground battle in New Guinea.

In another sector, the 2/12th Infantry Battalion commenced its movement from Waigani, positioning themselves to enter the fray later as a counter-offensive unit. Alongside the 2/9th, they were designated to strike from No. 3 Airstrip towards KB Mission. Concurrently, the Japanese repositioned their forces. Mikawa resolved to bolster the troops already on land. The supplemental forces from the 3rd Kure SNLF and 5th Yokosuka SNLF departed Rabaul on 28 August. That afternoon, an RAAF patrol identified the Japanese fleet, prompting Allied leaders to believe an imminent landing was at hand. Consequently, Clowes put a halt to his counter-offensive plans involving the 18th Brigade. In anticipation of a potential Japanese breakthrough, 30 Kittyhawks from Gili Gili were redirected to Port Moresby but returned the following morning.

On the evening of 29 August, the Japanese fleet neared Waga Waga, initiating troop and supply deployment while bombarding Allied defenses near Gili Gili. Despite this show of force, the bombardment yielded no significant damage or casualties. Throughout 30 August, Australian units undertook reconnaissance missions, while Japanese troops regrouped in the forest, prepping for a nocturnal assault.

As darkness enveloped the landscape, Japanese forces started assembling by No. 3 Airstrip's eastern edge. At 3:00 am on 31 August, they surged forward. However, the Australian troops, fortified by the 25th and 61st Infantry Battalions and the 46th Engineer General Service Regiment, fended off this initial assault with a barrage of machine gun, mortar, and artillery fire. Undeterred, the Japanese launched two more frenzied assaults, both of which met devastating resistance, leading to significant losses, including their commander, Hayashi. Subsequently, Commander Minoru Yano, who had recently arrived with reinforcements, assumed leadership. He attempted a flanking maneuver around the 61st Infantry Battalion's defenses but met staunch resistance from an Australian platoon equipped with Bren light machine guns. As dawn approached, a bugle's haunting notes signaled the Japanese retreat. Those who survived were taken aback by the formidable firepower displayed by the Allies, leaving the Japanese assault force fragmented and disoriented.

On the morning of 31 August, the 2/12th Infantry Battalion initiated their advance towards KB Mission. Leading the procession, 'D' Company faced challenging terrains made worse by torrential rains. Around 9:00 am, after bypassing the 61st Infantry Battalion's spot, they began a counterassault along Milne Bay's northern coast. Throughout their advance, they dealt with sniper attacks and ambushes. Some Japanese soldiers, feigning death, tried to deceive the Australians, leading to some Australians resorting to confirmatory measures to ensure the Japanese were dead. By midday, two companies from the 9th Infantry Battalion, a Militia division from the 7th Infantry Brigade, were dispatched to reclaim grounds around No. 3 Airstrip and the mission.

Despite facing heavy resistance, the Australians managed to reach KB Mission by evening, where they clashed with the remaining Japanese forces, resulting in 60 Japanese casualties. The Australians then secured their position at the mission. Meanwhile, two 9th Battalion companies positioned themselves at Kilarbo and between Gama River and Homo Creek, readying for the 2/12th's subsequent advance.

That same night, an estimated 300 Japanese soldiers, who had previously been pushed back by the 61st Infantry Battalion on Stephen's Ridge, confronted the 2/12th and 9th Infantry Battalions' defenses near Gama River. The Australians' counterassault led to approximately 90 Japanese casualties. The Japanese then employed stealth tactics, trying to navigate past Australian listening posts. Concurrently, at the mission, starting at around 8:00 pm, they engaged in diversionary tactics to assist their forces attempting to break Australian defenses at the Gama River, which persisted throughout the night.

On 1 September, the 2/12th Infantry Battalion resumed their offensive. Simultaneously, a squadron of seven Kittyhawks targeted the Japanese base near Waga Waga. By then, the Japanese shifted their goal from seizing airfields to merely fending off the Australians until evacuation. Unaware of this change in Japanese objectives, the Allies braced for another Japanese offensive. Due to an inaccurate intel report from MacArthur's headquarters, the 2/9th's assistance to the 2/12th was delayed by a day, as it prompted Clowes to adopt a short-term defensive strategy. However, when no attack materialized, the 2/9th was transported to the KB Mission on 2 September. By the following day, they took over from the 2/12th, spearheading the Australian progression.

In this region of the bay, the landscape was strategically advantageous for defenders due to numerous creeks that hindered movement and limited visibility for firing. On 3 September, the 2/9th Infantry Battalion faced significant obstacles. During a mid-morning skirmish near a stream west of Elevada Creek, they encountered a loss of 34 men as they tried to cross. Encountering heavy machine gun fire, the battalion retreated, only to discover later that the Japanese had left the area, leaving behind approximately 20 casualties.

Subsequently, the 2/9th progressed about 500 yards to Sanderson's Bay and set up camp for the night. Japanese vessels bombarded the Australian positions that evening, but didn't inflict any harm on the Australian troops.

The next day, 4 September, the 2/9th resumed their coastal advance. About an hour in, they met a Japanese stronghold at Goroni. The Australians strategized throughout the day and launched an attack at 3:15 pm. During this, a section of the 2/9th got pinned down by three Japanese machine gun posts. Corporal John French took the initiative, directing his section to take cover while he single-handedly attacked two machine gun posts using grenades. Braving the onslaught, he assaulted the third post with his Thompson submachine gun. When the rest of the section moved forward, they discovered the machine gun crew was eliminated, but French had tragically lost his life. For his valiant efforts and selflessness, he was posthumously awarded the Victoria Cross.

By the close of 4 September, the remaining Japanese force was significantly weakened. Out of their troops, only 50 were in fighting condition. The rest were either injured or could barely put up a defense. Additionally, leadership within the Japanese ranks had been devastated with company commanders lost and only a few platoon leaders remaining.

After the confrontations on 31 August, the Japanese units on the ground relayed the situation to their command center in Rabaul. As a countermeasure, the high command decided to dispatch the Aoba Detachment, consisting of the Army's 4th Infantry Regiment and an artillery company, to Rabi with the aim to secure the airfield. This reinforcement was slated to arrive on 11 September. In the interim, they planned to boost Yano's troops with an additional 130 soldiers from the 5th Yokosuka SNLF. Attempts to land these soldiers on 2 September and again on 4 September proved unsuccessful. Receiving updated reports from the frontlines, it became evident to the Japanese command that Yano's forces wouldn't be able to resist until the Aoba Detachment's arrival. Consequently, a decision to retreat was made on 5 September, which was executed that same night from the coast.

On the Allied side, 5 September witnessed the arrival of six Beauforts from No. 100 Squadron RAAF at Milne Bay, with three Beaufighters from No. 30 Squadron RAAF joining them a day later. These Beauforts were designated to provide supplementary resistance against potential landings and engage in anti-vessel operations. The subsequent day, 6 September, saw the Allies advancing to the primary base of the Japanese landing unit. During this push, they engaged in various minor skirmishes against remnants of the Japanese forces left behind after their evacuation.

On the evening of 6 September, just after 10 pm, the cargo ship Anshun was in the process of unloading its cargo when Japanese cruiser Tenryū and destroyer Arashi attacked. The Anshun was hit approximately ten times by the cruiser, causing it to tilt onto its side. Besides targeting the freighter, the Japanese vessels also aimed at onshore sites at Gili Gili and Waga Waga. Remarkably, the hospital ship Manunda, despite being brightly lit and clearly displaying its hospital ship markers, was spared from the attack. The following night, Australian positions faced another 15-minute barrage from two Japanese naval ships - a cruiser and a destroyer. This bombardment marked the Japanese naval forces' last action in the battle. In the aftermath, Australian forces conducted operations to locate and neutralize Japanese soldiers attempting to journey on foot to Buna.

Meanwhile, a stranded Japanese force of 350 troops on Goodenough Island, isolated since 24 August, remained trapped until late October. An evacuation attempt on 11 September failed, as USAAF aircraft attacked the two destroyers tasked with the rescue, resulting in the sinking of Yayoi. Although subsequent rescue attempts on 13 and 22 September didn't succeed, supplies were air-dropped to the trapped forces. On two occasions in October, a submarine managed to deliver additional supplies and evacuate 50 ailing personnel. Preparing for an assault on Buna and Gona, the 2/12th Infantry Battalion was tasked to secure Goodenough Island on 19 October. They landed there by 22 October, facing small skirmishes on 23 and 24 October. These confrontations led to 13 Australian casualties and 19 injuries, while the Japanese lost 20 soldiers and had 15 injured. The surviving Japanese soldiers were finally evacuated to Fergusson Island on the night of 24 October, and two days later, the cruiser Tenryū came to their rescue. With the island secured, the 2/12th focused on constructing the Vivigani Airfield along the eastern coast.

Battle of the Santa Cruz Islands

On 8 August 1942, Allied forces, mainly from the U.S., embarked on a mission to liberate the Japanese-held territories of Guadalcanal, Tulagi, and the Florida Islands in the Solomon Islands. This offensive aimed to prevent Japan from using these islands as strategic bases to disrupt supply routes between the U.S. and Australia. Additionally, the Allies wanted to establish a foundation for their campaign targeting the crucial Japanese base at Rabaul and support operations in New Guinea. This marked the onset of the six-month Guadalcanal campaign.

Following the Eastern Solomons Battle from 24–25 August, the USS Enterprise aircraft carrier suffered significant damage, prompting its return to Pearl Harbor, Hawaii for extensive repairs. However, three other U.S. carrier task forces stayed in the South Pacific, centered around the aircraft carriers USS Wasp, Saratoga, and Hornet. Accompanied by their respective air groups and various support vessels, including battleships, cruisers, and destroyers, these forces predominantly operated between the Solomons and New Hebrides (present-day Vanuatu). Their main tasks included safeguarding the communication line connecting major Allied bases in New Caledonia and Espiritu Santo, backing the Allied troops in Guadalcanal and Tulagi against potential Japanese attacks, ensuring the safe passage of supply vessels to Guadalcanal, and confronting and eliminating Japanese naval forces, particularly aircraft carriers, within their vicinity. The waters where the U.S. task forces operated became notoriously known as "Torpedo Junction" due to the prevalence of Japanese submarines.

Regrettably, on 31 August, a Japanese submarine, I-26, torpedoed Saratoga, putting it out of commission for three months. A more dire situation arose on 15 September when Wasp, while aiding a significant reinforcement convoy to Guadalcanal and almost confronting the Japanese carriers Shōkaku and Zuikaku, was struck by three torpedoes from the Japanese submarine I-19. The torpedo hits severely disrupted Wasp's power, and with damage-control teams unable to control the subsequent fires, it was decided to abandon and scuttle the ship.

Even though the U.S. was left with just the Hornet carrier operational in the South Pacific, the Allies still held aerial dominance over the southern Solomon Islands, thanks to their planes stationed at Henderson Field on Guadalcanal. Yet, the nights posed a challenge. In the darkness, when planes couldn't function efficiently, the Japanese navigated their vessels around Guadalcanal with minimal obstruction. This led to a standstill in the Guadalcanal conflict. The Allies would bring in supplies and reinforcements during daylight, while the Japanese, using their warships nicknamed the "Tokyo Express" by the Allies, would do the same after sunset. Neither side could transport ample forces to the island to achieve a clear upper hand. By the middle of October, the forces were almost evenly split on the island.

This impasse was briefly disrupted by two significant naval confrontations. On the night of 11–12 October, a U.S. naval brigade clashed with and overpowered a Japanese brigade intending to strike Henderson Field, in what became known as the Battle of Cape Esperance. However, just two nights afterwards, Japanese forces, which included the powerful battleships Haruna and Kongō, managed to bombard Henderson Field successfully. This assault destroyed most of the U.S. planes stationed there and heavily damaged the field's infrastructure.

The U.S. strategized two key initiatives to shift the balance in the Guadalcanal battle. First, they hastened the repair works on the Enterprise so it could rejoin the South Pacific theater swiftly. By 10 October, the Enterprise was equipped with its new Air Group 10. On 16 October, she departed Pearl Harbor, and by 23 October, she had made her way back to the South Pacific, meeting up with Hornet and other Allied naval forces northeast of Espiritu Santo by 24 October.

In a second significant move, on 18 October, Admiral Chester Nimitz, the Allied Pacific Forces' Commander-in-Chief, appointed Vice Admiral William Halsey, Jr. to replace Vice Admiral Robert L. Ghormley as the South Pacific Area Commander, overseeing the Solomon Islands campaign. Nimitz believed Ghormley's perspective had become too narrow and negative for the Guadalcanal campaign. Halsey was renowned within the U.S. naval community for his combative spirit.

Simultaneously, the Japanese Combined Fleet was gearing up for what they hoped would be a game-changing confrontation. In early October, two fleet carriers, Hiyō and Jun'yō, alongside the light carrier Zuihō, joined Shōkaku and Zuikaku at Truk Atoll, the central Japanese naval base. Boasting five carriers with complete air groups and an array of battleships, cruisers, and destroyers, Admiral Isoroku Yamamoto's Japanese Combined Fleet was optimistic about avenging their defeat at the Battle of Midway. Although they conducted sporadic air raids on Henderson Field in October, the Japanese carriers primarily stayed in the Solomon Islands' northwestern region, away from the Guadalcanal frontline, ready to counteract U.S. carriers. As the Japanese Army planned a significant ground assault on Allied forces in Guadalcanal for 20 October, Yamamoto's fleet began navigating towards the southern Solomons. Their objective was to support the upcoming offensive and to confront any incoming enemy vessels, particularly U.S. carriers, bolstering the Allied defense of Guadalcanal.

Around 11 October, a significant naval force, including aircraft carriers and battleships with their escorts, set sail from Truk to support the October offensive in Guadalcanal. That same day, a pivotal reinforcement convoy reached Guadalcanal. However, a group of heavy cruisers intended to attack Henderson Field was intercepted and repelled in an engagement known as the

Battle of Cape Esperance. Subsequently, between 13 and 16 October, the naval forces conducted three intense bombardment missions against the airfield, marking the most aggressive naval assault on the airstrip throughout the campaign. Notably, two of these bombardments involved ships from Vice Admiral Nobutake Kondō's Advance Force.

On the night of 14 October, a crucial convoy carrying four transports managed to unload most of their cargo, which included tanks and heavy artillery. On 15 October, while guiding the tug Vireo with a supply barge, the destroyer Meredith was detected and destroyed by planes from the carriers Zuikaku and Shokaku. On 17 October, the carriers Hiyō and Jun'yō dispatched an airstrike targeting transports near Lunga Point, but inflicted no harm. This formidable fleet continued its presence around Guadalcanal until the conclusion of the Battle of the Santa Cruz Islands, after which they retreated to Truk by October's end. Although the newly commissioned carrier Hiyō was initially with the fleet, an engineering room fire on 21 October necessitated her withdrawal to Truk for repairs. On 25 October, a squadron from Jun'yo, consisting of 6 bombers and 12 fighters, targeted Henderson Field but caused minimal destruction.

Between 20 and 25 October, Japanese ground forces launched an aggressive assault to seize Henderson Field from its U.S. defenders. However, their efforts were firmly repelled, resulting in significant losses for the Japanese. Misjudging the situation and assuming they had captured Henderson Field, on 25 October, the Japanese dispatched naval vessels from the Shortland Islands towards Guadalcanal to back their ground forces. However, planes from Henderson Field fiercely engaged the convoy, leading to the sinking of the light cruiser Yura, assisted by B-17s from Espiritu Santo, and inflicted damage on the destroyer Akizuki.

Even with the setbacks on the ground and the sinking of Yura, the Combined Fleet persisted in its attempts to engage Allied naval forces in combat around the southern Solomon Islands on 25 October. The Japanese naval composition at this point consisted of four carriers (two of them being large-scale, one medium, and one light), given Hiyō's prior exit. This force had the combined strength of roughly three Shokaku-class fleet carriers in terms of aircraft.

The Japanese naval configuration was split into three main groups:

1. The "Advanced" force, led by Kondō aboard the heavy cruiser Atago, had Jun'yō, four heavy cruisers, a light cruiser, and seven destroyers. Supporting this force was Rear Admiral Takeo Kurita, commanding two battleships and a pair of destroyers.
2. Vice Admiral Chūichi Nagumo commanded the "Main Body" from aboard Shōkaku. This group included carriers Shōkaku, Zuikaku, and Zuihō, along with a heavy cruiser and eight destroyers.
3. The "Vanguard" force was spearheaded by Rear Admiral Hiroaki Abe aboard the battleship Hiei. This contingent included two battleships, three heavy cruisers, a light cruiser, and seven destroyers.

Besides leading the Advanced force, Kondo also held the overarching command of all three units.

From the U.S. perspective, the Hornet and Enterprise task groups, under the collective leadership of Rear Admiral Thomas Kinkaid, were positioned to the north of the Santa Cruz Islands on 25 October, in hopes of encountering the Japanese naval units. The American ships were organized into two distinct carrier groups with a separation of around 12 mi. An American PBY Catalina scout plane based in the Santa Cruz Islands detected the Japanese Main Body carriers at 11:03. The distance between the Japanese carriers and the U.S. force was about 409 mi, slightly beyond the range of carrier-based aircraft. To bridge this gap and potentially launch a successful assault that day, Kinkaid pushed his fleet towards the Japanese at maximum speed, deploying a 23-aircraft strike force by 14:25. However, the Japanese fleet, aware of their detection and uncertain about the U.S. carriers' location, shifted northward to maintain distance. Consequently, the U.S. strike team returned without locating or engaging the Japanese naval forces.

On the early morning of 26 October at 02:50, Japanese naval units made a course reversal. By 05:00, both the Japanese and the U.S. fleets had drawn closer, with a mere 230 mi separating them. Anticipating conflict, both sides dispatched reconnaissance planes and readied their strike aircraft for engagement once the opponent's location was confirmed. Although a radar-fitted Catalina had already spotted the Japanese carriers at 03:10, this crucial information didn't reach Kinkaid until 05:12. Given the time lapse, Kinkaid assumed the Japanese fleet had repositioned. He opted to delay any immediate strike, choosing to wait for updated intelligence on the Japanese fleet's whereabouts.

Around 06:45, American reconnaissance identified Nagumo's primary carrier fleet. Barely minutes later, at 06:58, the U.S. Hornet's task force was spotted by a Japanese scout. With both sides alerted, a race commenced to strike first. By 07:40, the Japanese had already launched a formidable 64-aircraft assault directed at Hornet.

Concurrently, Kondo directed Abe's Vanguard to speed ahead, aiming to engage the American fleet directly. Also moving at full throttle, Kondo's Advanced force aimed to position Jun'yō's planes for assault on the U.S. vessels. By 09:10, the Japanese dispatched over 100 aircraft toward the U.S. carriers.

In contrast, U.S. strike planes lagged approximately 20 minutes behind. Prioritizing a swift offensive over a coordinated massed attack, American aircraft advanced in smaller detachments. The initial American formation, led by Lieutenant Commander Widhelm from Hornet, departed around 08:00. The subsequent groups followed shortly after, launching in intervals.

By 08:40, the two sides' aerial forces crossed paths. Japanese Zeros from Zuihō ambushed the Enterprise group. A fierce dogfight ensued, resulting in several downed planes on both sides. Having used up their ammunition, the remaining Zuihō Zeros then pulled out of the confrontation.

Around 08:50, Hornet's leading U.S. strike group identified a quartet of vessels from Abe's Vanguard fleet. Pushing forward, they soon laid eyes on the Japanese carriers and readied their assault. However, they faced interference: three Zuihō Zeros engaged the Wildcats, distracting them from guarding the bombers. Consequently, the dive bombers commenced their descent without fighter protection. A dozen Zeros from the Japanese aerial defense swooped in, shooting down two bombers and causing two others to abandon their attack. Nonetheless, 11 of the bombers managed to target Shōkaku by 09:27, landing between three to six hits, which rendered significant damage to the carrier's flight deck and interior. One stray bomber mistook its target, narrowly missing Japanese destroyer Teruzuki. The six torpedo planes from the first U.S. group, having lost their way, couldn't locate the Japanese carriers and redirected towards Hornet. During their return, they launched an unsuccessful attack on the Japanese heavy cruiser Tone, with all torpedoes missing their mark.

The Enterprise's second U.S. attack group of TBFs couldn't pinpoint the Japanese carriers. Instead, they targeted the Japanese heavy cruiser Suzuya from Abe's Vanguard, though they inflicted no harm. Concurrently, nine SBDs from Hornet's third U.S. group zeroed in on Abe's fleet and bombarded the Japanese heavy cruiser Chikuma. Two direct hits and subsequent attacks from other Enterprise SBDs inflicted substantial damage to the cruiser. Following this, the third group's TBFs joined the assault, securing another hit on Chikuma. Consequently, with two destroyers as escorts, the wounded Chikuma retreated from the battlefront, moving towards Truk for mending.

By 08:30, the U.S. carrier squadrons were alerted by their outbound planes about the oncoming Japanese strike force. By 08:52, the Japanese strike commander located the Hornet fleet, while the Enterprise group remained shielded by a rainstorm. Preparing for the imminent assault, the Japanese planes geared up for action. At 08:55, the U.S. carriers, using radar, detected the approaching Japanese fleet about 40 mi out. The U.S. immediately dispatched 37 Wildcats from their Combat Air Patrol (CAP) to confront the Japanese planes. Yet, due to communication breakdowns, rudimentary control processes, and errors by the U.S. fighter directors, most Wildcats couldn't engage the Japanese planes before they initiated their assault on the Hornet. Despite these challenges, a few U.S. CAP managed to shoot down or impair several dive bombers, though many Japanese planes initiated their attack relatively unhindered.

At 09:09, Hornet's anti-aircraft defenses and those of her accompanying vessels sprang to action as the 20 Japanese torpedo planes and 16 dive bombers, which had remained unscathed, began their assault on the carrier. At 09:12, a precise dive bomber strike sent a 250 kg semi-armor-piercing bomb crashing through Hornet's flight deck, detonating after penetrating three decks, taking the lives of 60 men. Shortly after, another bomb, weighing 242 kg, exploded on impact, creating a sizable hole and killing 30 crew members. A third bomb soon hit close to the initial impact site, causing considerable damage, albeit without fatalities. By 09:14, Hornet's defenses set a dive bomber ablaze. The pilot, Warrant Officer Shigeyuki Sato, in a final act, aimed his stricken plane into Hornet's stack, spreading fiery fuel and killing seven crew members.

Simultaneously, the 20 torpedo bombers zeroed in on Hornet from various angles. Even as many were shot down, including their leader, Murata, two torpedoes struck Hornet between 09:13 and 09:17, disabling her propulsion. With the carrier immobilized, a damaged Japanese dive bomber made a deliberate crash on the carrier, igniting a fire near its main aviation fuel storage. By 09:20, the remaining Japanese aircraft disengaged, leaving Hornet stationary and aflame. The attack resulted in the loss of 25 Japanese and six U.S. planes, comprising 12 dive bombers, ten torpedo bombers, and at least one fighter.

By 10:00, with support from three nearby destroyers, Hornet's fires were contained. Injured crew members were transferred off the ship. USS Northampton, under Captain Willard A. Kitts, endeavored to tow Hornet away from the ongoing battle. But setting up the tow was time-consuming, and additional waves of Japanese aircraft were fast approaching.

By 09:30, Enterprise started receiving many of the fuel-starved CAP fighters and reconnaissance aircraft from both carriers. But with her flight deck becoming crowded and another wave of Japanese planes spotted on radar at 09:30, landing operations on Enterprise were halted at 10:00. Consequently, aircraft low on fuel had to ditch into the sea, with the carrier's escort destroyers moving in to retrieve the aircrews. In one such rescue attempt, a damaged TBF from Enterprise, which had been previously attacked by Zeros from Zuihō, went down close to the USS Porter. As the crew of the Porter worked to save the TBF's aircrew, a torpedo struck the destroyer, resulting in significant damage and the death of 15 sailors. Given the extent of the damage, the decision was made to scuttle the Porter. Its crew was then saved by the USS Shaw, which subsequently delivered the final blows to sink the stricken Porter.

When the initial wave of Japanese aircraft started returning to their carriers after targeting Hornet, they noticed the Enterprise task force emerging from the protective cover of the rain squall and promptly relayed its position. This prompted the second wave of Japanese strike aircraft to shift their focus to the Enterprise task force, initiating their attack around 10:08. Unfortunately, the U.S. CAP found it challenging to fend off the Japanese planes before they could strike, managing to down just 2 out of the 19 dive bombers.

The onslaught from the Japanese aircraft was relentless, with Seki's team diving first, although they failed to land any hits. Arima's division followed, successfully landing two 250 kg semi-armor-piercing bombs on the Enterprise. These strikes resulted in the deaths of 44 crewmen and left 75 injured. The carrier also sustained considerable damage, including a jammed forward elevator. This attack saw the loss of ten Japanese bombers, with two more being forced to ditch on their return.

By 10:28, the 16 torpedo planes from Zuikaku entered the fray, splitting their focus on the Enterprise. Some of them caught the attention of two CAP Wildcats, with Vejtasa once again demonstrating his prowess by downing three and critically damaging a fourth. This damaged aircraft, ablaze and spiraling, intentionally crashed into the destroyer Smith, sparking a blaze that claimed the lives of 57 crew members. The onboard torpedo exploded soon after, inflicting further damage. Initially, the situation looked bleak, but a quick decision by Smith's captain to navigate into the spraying wake of the battleship USS South Dakota helped extinguish the flames. After this ordeal, Smith returned to her post, ready to repel further attacks.

The subsequent attack by the remaining torpedo planes on Enterprise, South Dakota, and the cruiser Portland proved futile, with all torpedoes either missing their mark or malfunctioning, resulting in no harm. The onslaught subsided by 10:53, with the Japanese losing 9 out of the 16 torpedo aircraft involved in the attack. At 11:15, with most of the fires onboard the Enterprise contained, the ship readied to welcome back its aircraft from the earlier morning strikes on Japanese naval forces. This brief respite was short-lived, as yet another wave of Japanese aircraft soon appeared, compelling the suspension of landing operations.

From 09:05 to 09:14, the Jun'yō had positioned itself within 280 nautical miles of the U.S. carriers and dispatched a strike force of 17 dive bombers and 12 Zeros, led by Lieutenant Yoshio Shiga. As the primary Japanese fleet and the advanced force coordinated their movements, Jun'yō prepared for additional strikes. At 11:21, the Jun'yō's aircraft descended on the Enterprise task force. The dive bombers managed to secure a near hit on the Enterprise, further damaging the carrier, and successfully targeted South Dakota and light cruiser San Juan, causing notable damage. This assault saw the loss of eight of the seventeen Japanese dive bombers, with another three forced to make emergency landings.

By 11:35, the situation had grown dire. With the Hornet incapacitated, Enterprise critically damaged, and the looming threat of potentially one or two unscathed Japanese carriers nearby, Kinkaid deemed it wise to pull the Enterprise and its protective vessels out of the conflict. The decision was made to leave the beleaguered Hornet and guide the Enterprise and its task force to safety. Between 11:39 and 13:22, as Enterprise beat a hasty retreat, she managed to recover 57 of the 73 airborne U.S. aircraft. The other U.S. aircraft were left with no choice but to land in the sea, with their crews subsequently rescued by the accompanying ships.

From 11:40 to 14:00, the two untouched Japanese carriers, Zuikaku and Jun'yō, facilitated the return of the few aircraft that had participated in the morning raids on Hornet and Enterprise. These carriers then began preparations for potential subsequent strikes.

At 13:00, Kondo's Advanced force and Abe's Vanguard force ships set their course straight to the last known location of the U.S. carrier task forces, accelerating to possibly engage in a direct naval gunfight. The wounded carriers, Zuihō and Shōkaku, with Nagumo still onboard, pulled back from the combat zone. The responsibility of leading the Zuikaku and Jun'yō aircraft divisions now rested on Rear Admiral Kakuji Kakuta. At 13:06, Jun'yō set off her second wave, comprising seven torpedo planes headed by Lieutenant Yoshiaki Irikiin, guarded by eight Zeros under the command of Lieutenant Shirane. Simultaneously, Zuikaku dispatched her third wave, which included seven torpedo planes, two dive bombers, and five Zeros, led by Lieutenant Ichirō Tanaka. Notably, the majority of the torpedo planes were equipped with an 800 kg armor-piercing bomb. At 15:35, marking the final Japanese aerial attack for the day, Jun'yō deployed a squad made up of four dive bombers and six Zeros, once again under Lieutenant Shiga's command.

Facing numerous technical issues, the Northampton managed to start towing the Hornet away from the battleground at 14:45, but at a sluggish pace of merely five knots. The Hornet's crew was nearing the completion of partial power restoration when at 15:20, Jun'yō's second strike team approached. Among the seven torpedo planes, one was successful in hitting Hornet directly in the middle at 15:23. This blow proved catastrophic, annihilating the power system repair progress and causing extensive flooding, leading to a pronounced 14-degree tilt. With the power out, there was no means to drain the flooding, leading to the decision to abandon the stricken Hornet. The subsequent strike from Zuikaku also targeted the sinking Hornet, hitting it with an 800 kg bomb. By 16:27, all of Hornet's crew had evacuated. Later that day, Jun'yō's third strike team landed one last blow with a 250 kg semi-AP bomb on the sinking ship.

Upon learning that enemy forces were nearing and that further towing attempts were futile, Halsey ordered Hornet to be scuttled. As the bulk of the U.S. fleet moved southeastward, out of reach from Kondō's and Abe's advancing forces, destroyers USS Mustin and Anderson tried but failed to sink the Hornet using torpedoes and extensive gunfire. With Japanese forces drawing closer, the two destroyers left the burning Hornet by 20:40. By 22:20, Kondō's and Abe's fleet reached Hornet's site. Japanese destroyers Makigumo and Akigumo finally sank Hornet using four 24 torpedoes, and by 01:35 on 27 October 1942, she was submerged at roughly 08°38′S 166°43′E. The U.S. fleet's head start in their departure, combined with several nighttime attacks by Catalinas on Jun'yō and Teruzuki and fuel constraints, seemingly deterred the Japanese from further pursuing the U.S. ships. After refueling near the northern Solomon Islands, the Japanese fleet returned to Truk on 30 October. As the U.S. retreated, South Dakota collided with the destroyer Mahan while dodging a Japanese submarine, causing significant damage to the latter.

Both the Americans and Japanese declared themselves victors. The U.S. claimed to have damaged and neutralized two Shōkaku-class fleet carriers. Kinkaid also reported hits on a battleship, three heavy cruisers, a light cruiser, and suspected damage to another heavy cruiser. In truth, only Shōkaku, Zuihō, and Chikuma sustained hits, but none sank. The Japanese, on the other hand, believed they had destroyed three U.S. carriers, a battleship, a cruiser, a destroyer, and an additional "unidentified large warship". The actual American casualties were the carrier Hornet, the destroyer Porter, and damages to Enterprise, San Juan, Smith, and South Dakota.

Hornet's loss was a significant setback for the Allies in the South Pacific, leaving only Enterprise and Saratoga as functional Allied carriers in the Pacific. As Enterprise pulled away from the fray, a banner on the flight deck boldly declared: "Enterprise vs Japan". Though she was not fully restored after receiving provisional repairs in New Caledonia, Enterprise was back in the southern Solomons within two weeks, aiding the Allies in the Naval Battle of Guadalcanal. There, her aircraft played a pivotal role, sinking several Japanese naval vessels and transports near Henderson Field. The scarcity of carriers compelled both sides to deploy battleships for nighttime operations around Guadalcanal. This was a rare instance in the Pacific War where battleships directly engaged, resulting in damages to South Dakota and the loss of two Japanese battleships.

Despite the Japanese having an edge in the Battle of Santa Cruz regarding ships sunk, they paid a hefty price. Jun'yō was the lone aircraft carrier left to confront Enterprise or Henderson Field for the rest of the Guadalcanal campaign. Although Zuikaku remained undamaged and managed to recover aircraft from the two impaired carriers, she was redeployed to the home islands via Truk for training and transporting aircraft, not returning to the South Pacific until February 1943 to oversee the evacuation of Japanese troops from Guadalcanal. The damaged carriers, Zuihō and Shōkaku, needed extensive repairs in Japan. Zuihō was operational again by late January 1943, while Shōkaku's repairs extended till March 1943, with her return to the front lines only in July 1943, rejoining Zuikaku at Truk.

Operation Torch

The Allies formulated a plan for an Anglo-American assault on French North Africa, encompassing the regions of Morocco, Algeria, and Tunisia, which were ostensibly under the control of the Vichy French regime. This strategic move was intended to complement the British forces pushing forward from Egypt, aiming to envelop the Axis powers in North Africa in a pincer maneuver. The Vichy French possessed a military presence of approximately 125,000 troops across these territories, supported by coastal artillery, a fleet of 210 tanks that were outdated, and around 500 aircraft, with half of them being Dewoitine D.520 fighters—a match for many of the fighters in the British and U.S. fleets. The distribution of their forces included 60,000 soldiers stationed in Morocco, 15,000 in Tunisia, and 50,000 in Algeria, along with their respective artillery, a modest assortment of tanks, and a few aircraft. The naval capacity at Casablanca comprised about 10 warships and 11 submarines.

The Allies held the view that the Vichy French forces, bound by an armistice, were unlikely to engage in combat, a belief partly informed by intelligence from the American Consul in Algiers, Robert Daniel Murphy. Since the French had previously been allies and considering the presence of American forces, the directive given to the U.S. troops was to hold fire unless attacked. Nevertheless, there was an underlying concern that the Vichy French Naval forces might seek retribution for the British assault on the French fleet at Mers-el-Kébir, near Oran, in June 1940—an offensive that resulted in the deaths of nearly 1,300 French sailors, to prevent the ships from falling into

German hands.

Understanding the loyalty of the French forces in North Africa was critical; therefore, efforts were focused on ensuring their support or at least their non-resistance. On the German side, assistance to the Vichy French was primarily in the form of aerial reinforcement. Luftwaffe bomber squadrons carried out strikes aimed at disrupting Allied shipping and targeted ports in Algiers and other locations along the North African coastline.

Initially, General Joseph Stilwell was slated to command the operation, but his pronounced dislike for the British and doubts about the mission led to his reassignment following the insights from the Arcadia Conference. Consequently, Lt. General Dwight D. Eisenhower was appointed to take over the leadership of the operation, establishing his command center in Gibraltar. The responsibility for the Allied Naval Expeditionary Force fell to Admiral Sir Andrew Cunningham, with Vice-Admiral Sir Bertram Ramsay serving as his second-in-command, orchestrating the amphibious assault plans.

The operation's strategists pinpointed Oran, Algiers, and Casablanca as critical objectives. Ideally, they also wanted a landing at Tunis to seize control of Tunisia and cut off the supply routes to Erwin Rommel's Afrika Korps in Italian Libya. However, Tunis's proximity to Axis-controlled airfields in Sicily and Sardinia rendered such a direct assault too perilous. As a middle ground, Bône in eastern Algeria, roughly 300 miles from Tunis and closer than Algiers, emerged as a viable alternative. Due to limited resources, the Allies were constrained to three primary landings. Eisenhower, committed to ensuring that Oran and Algiers were among the landing sites, faced a choice: He could opt for the western approach, capturing Casablanca, Oran, and Algiers and then advancing swiftly to Tunis, or he could take the eastern route, targeting Oran, Algiers, and Bône, and then proceeding to Casablanca. Preferring the latter for the strategic benefit of an early Tunis capture and due to the hazardous Atlantic swells at Casablanca, which posed a significant threat to amphibious operations compared to the calmer Mediterranean conditions.

Nonetheless, the Combined Chiefs of Staff were wary of the political ramifications, particularly if Operation Torch triggered Spain to forsake its neutrality and side with the Axis, potentially jeopardizing access to the Mediterranean through the closure of the Straits of Gibraltar. They selected the Casablanca landing, reasoning that even if the straits were blocked, supplies could still be transported overland from Casablanca to forces in Algeria and Tunisia, despite the logistical challenges this might entail.

Marshall's reservations about Torch not only postponed the invasion by nearly a month but his reluctance towards landings in Algeria also led to British skepticism over his strategic insight; the Royal Navy's dominion over the Strait of Gibraltar and Spain's calculated neutrality under Franco made intervention unlikely. The decision for Morocco landings compromised the swift occupation of Tunisia. Marshall succeeded in persuading the Allies to dismiss any plans to invade Madeira and Tangier, arguing they would sacrifice the element of surprise and possibly draw Spanish forces into the conflict. However, Harry Hopkins swayed President Franklin D. Roosevelt to sanction the overall strategy. During this period, Eisenhower confided to Patton that it was the most taxing six weeks of his life. By consenting to the landings in Algeria and Morocco, Eisenhower acknowledged that it significantly diminished the chances of quickly capturing Tunis, affording the Axis more time to reinforce their presence in Tunisia.

The operation's strategists pinpointed Oran, Algiers, and Casablanca as critical objectives. Ideally, they also wanted a landing at Tunis to seize control of Tunisia and cut off the supply routes to Erwin Rommel's Afrika Korps in Italian Libya. However, Tunis's proximity to Axis-controlled airfields in Sicily and Sardinia rendered such a direct assault too perilous. As a middle ground, Bône in eastern Algeria, roughly 300 miles from Tunis and closer than Algiers, emerged as a viable alternative. Due to limited resources, the Allies were constrained to three primary landings. Eisenhower, committed to ensuring that Oran and Algiers were among the landing sites, faced a choice: He could opt for the western approach, capturing Casablanca, Oran, and Algiers and then advancing swiftly to Tunis, or he could take the eastern route, targeting

Oran, Algiers, and Bône, and then proceeding to Casablanca. Preferring the latter for the strategic benefit of an early Tunis capture and due to the hazardous Atlantic swells at Casablanca, which posed a significant threat to amphibious operations compared to the calmer Mediterranean conditions.

Nonetheless, the Combined Chiefs of Staff were wary of the political ramifications, particularly if Operation Torch triggered Spain to forsake its neutrality and side with the Axis, potentially jeopardizing access to the Mediterranean through the closure of the Straits of Gibraltar. They selected the Casablanca landing, reasoning that even if the straits were blocked, supplies could still be transported overland from Casablanca to forces in Algeria and Tunisia, despite the logistical challenges this might entail.

Marshall's reservations about Torch not only postponed the invasion by nearly a month but his reluctance towards landings in Algeria also led to British skepticism over his strategic insight; the Royal Navy's dominion over the Strait of Gibraltar and Spain's calculated neutrality under Franco made intervention unlikely. The decision for Morocco landings compromised the swift occupation of Tunisia. Marshall succeeded in persuading the Allies to dismiss any plans to invade Madeira and Tangier, arguing they would sacrifice the element of surprise and possibly draw Spanish forces into the conflict. However, Harry Hopkins swayed President Franklin D. Roosevelt to sanction the overall strategy. During this period, Eisenhower confided to Patton that it was the most taxing six weeks of his life. By consenting to the landings in Algeria and Morocco, Eisenhower acknowledged that it significantly diminished the chances of quickly capturing Tunis, affording the Axis more time to reinforce their presence in Tunisia.

In July 1941, under the alias "Rygor"—the Polish term for "Rigor"—Mieczysław Słowikowski established "Agency Africa," which would become one of the most effective intelligence networks of the Second World War. Key figures aiding him in this effort were Lt. Col. Gwido Langer and Major Maksymilian Ciężki from Poland. The intelligence collected by this agency proved crucial for the American and British forces in strategizing the amphibious Operation Torch landings in North Africa that took place in November 1942.

To assess the stance of the Vichy French forces, Murphy was discreetly assigned to the American consulate in Algeria. His secret task involved discerning the sentiments of the French military and establishing connections with those who might be amenable to an Allied invasion. He managed to make contact with several French officers, among them General Charles Mast, the top French military official in Algiers.

These officers were open to backing the Allied cause but requested a secret meeting with a high-ranking Allied General on Algerian soil. To facilitate this, Major General Mark W. Clark, a senior aide to Eisenhower, covertly traveled to Cherchell in Algeria via the British submarine HMS Seraph, where he met with these Vichy French officers on October 21, 1942.

Additionally, with assistance from the French Resistance, the Allies covertly transported French General Henri Giraud from Vichy France to Gibraltar aboard HMS Seraph, which was masquerading as an American submarine, to present him with an offer from Eisenhower to lead French forces in North Africa post-invasion. Nonetheless, Giraud held out for a more prestigious role, specifically as the supreme commander of all invasion forces, a position Eisenhower already occupied. Upon being denied this role, Giraud opted to stay out of the operation.

The Allies orchestrated a three-pronged amphibious assault to capture strategic ports and airfields in Morocco and Algeria, focusing on Casablanca, Oran, and Algiers. The intent was that, once these areas were secured, forces would push east towards Tunisia.

The task force designated to take Casablanca, labeled the Western Task Force, was composed primarily of American military units. Major General George S. Patton led the ground troops, while Rear Admiral Henry Kent Hewitt commanded the naval components. This Western Task Force included the U.S. 3rd and 9th Infantry Divisions, along with two battalions from the U.S. 2nd Armored Division, amounting to 35,000 soldiers. These troops were part of a massive convoy of more than 100 ships that sailed directly from the United States, marking the beginning of a new sequence of UG convoys that would supply the North African campaign with necessary logistical support.

The Center Task Force, designated for the assault on Oran, was comprised of the U.S. 2nd Battalion 509th Parachute Infantry Regiment, the U.S. 1st Infantry Division, and the U.S. 1st Armored Division, summing up to 18,500 troops. This force embarked from the United Kingdom under the leadership of Major General Lloyd Fredendall, with the naval contingent under the direction of Commodore Thomas Troubridge.

Operation Torch was strategically presented as predominantly an American effort, accompanied by British naval and air support, based on the assumption that French public sentiment would be more receptive to an American-led operation rather than a joint Anglo-American invasion. In line with this approach, Churchill even proposed that British troops might don U.S. Army uniforms for the cause, a tactic actually employed by No.6 Commando. In support of this ruse, Fleet Air Arm planes carried the U.S. "star" insignia for the duration of the operation, and two British destroyers flew the Stars and Stripes.

However, in reality, the Eastern Task Force targeting Algiers was under the command of Lieutenant-General Kenneth Anderson. It consisted of a brigade each from the British 78th and the U.S. 34th Infantry Divisions, in addition to two British commando units (No. 1 and No. 6 Commandos), and included the RAF Regiment which provided both infantry squadrons and light anti-aircraft flights, totaling an operational force of 20,000 troops. During the initial landing, U.S. Major General Charles W. Ryder, from the 34th Division, took charge of ground operations, while Vice-Admiral Sir Harold Burrough of the Royal Navy led the naval forces.

To minimize the threat of U-boat attacks, the German submarines, usually patrolling the eastern Atlantic, were redirected to engage the trade convoy SL 125 instead. Air support duties were divided regionally: RAF aircraft, under the command of Air Marshal Sir William Welsh, operated to the east of Cape Tenez in Algeria, while the U.S. Army Air Forces, commanded by Major General Jimmy Doolittle and reporting directly to Major General Patton, operated to the west of Cape Tenez. Notably, P-40 fighters from the 33rd Fighter Group were launched from U.S. Navy escort carriers, successfully landing at Port Lyautey on November 10. The aircraft carrier USS Ranger also played a significant role, with its squadrons engaging Vichy French aircraft and targeting enemy vessels.

The Western Task Force commenced its operations in the early hours of November 8, 1942, targeting three sites in Morocco: Safi under Operation Blackstone, Fedala (where Operation Brushwood saw the primary influx of 19,000 men), and Mehdiya-Port Lyautey as part of Operation Goalpost. Anticipating minimal resistance, the Allied strategy did not include a pre-invasion bombardment, a decision that would result in unexpected losses due to entrenched French defensive positions.

On the eve of the invasion, November 7, General Antoine Béthouart, sympathetic to the Allied cause, initiated an insurrection against the French leadership in Morocco with the intention of yielding to the Allies upon their arrival. His units encircled the residence of General Charles Noguès, the staunch Vichy French commissioner. However, the plan faltered when Noguès managed to call upon faithful military elements who thwarted the putsch. Furthermore, this premature action tipped off Noguès about the imminent Allied offensive, prompting him to immediately reinforce the coastal fortifications.

In Fedala, near Casablanca, inclement weather complicated the landing efforts. Once the sun rose, French defenses began firing on the invading forces at the beach. General Patton made his landing at 08:00, and throughout the day, the beachheads were secured. By November 10, American forces had encircled Casablanca, which surrendered just as the Allies were preparing for a final offensive. Casablanca was significant as the primary French naval base on the Atlantic following the German occupation of European coastal areas. The Naval Battle of Casablanca ensued when French warships, including cruisers, destroyers, and submarines, sortied to oppose the landings. The Americans countered effectively, sinking a cruiser, six destroyers, and six submarines through naval artillery and aerial bombardment. The French battleship Jean Bart, though incomplete and immobile at the dock, engaged the invaders until it was put out of action by the USS Massachusetts, marking the first instance of American naval forces using 16-inch guns in the Second World War. The Jean Bart was later sunk by bombers, after numerous shells failed to detonate, likely due to faulty detonators. In this confrontation, two American destroyers sustained damage.

At Safi, the objective was to secure the port to disembark the medium tanks of the Western Task Force. The landings commenced without a preliminary barrage, under the hopeful assumption of no French resistance. Yet, when French coastal batteries began to engage, the Allied naval forces returned fire. By the time armored reinforcements arrived, French sharpshooters had already immobilized the first-wave assault troops on Safi's shores, with many landings falling behind schedule. Allied aircraft quickly neutralized a French convoy en route to reinforce beach defenses, and by the afternoon of November 8, Safi had capitulated. By November 10, the remaining French resistance was subdued, and the bulk of the Allied forces pivoted to aid in the Casablanca offensive.

At Port-Lyautey, navigational uncertainties and subsequent delays allowed French forces to organize a more robust defense, confronting the later waves of Allied troops with artillery fire. Innovative tactics, such as using a former French pilot to navigate a US destroyer up the shallow river, neutralized a key artillery position, paving the way for the airbase's capture. Supported by carrier-based air cover, the ground forces advanced and secured their targets, contributing to the broader objectives of the operation.

The Center Task Force faced challenges during its division across three beaches near Oran, with two positioned to the west and one to the east. The approach to the westernmost beach experienced delays due to an encounter with a French convoy during the minesweeping process. The landings were further complicated by unanticipated shallow waters and sandbars that caused confusion and some damage to the landing vessels. Despite prior periscope surveys, the lack of on-the-ground beach reconnaissance to assess maritime conditions led to these obstacles. The lessons learned from these difficulties were taken into account for future operations, such as Operation Overlord, where extensive pre-landing reconnaissance was deemed crucial.

The U.S. 1st Ranger Battalion successfully took control of the coastal battery at Arzew to the east of Oran. Concurrently, there was an effort to deploy U.S. infantry directly into the harbor with the intent of swiftly safeguarding the port infrastructure and averting the scuttling of French ships. This initiative, named Operation Reservist, was met with failure as the two involved Banff-class sloops encountered heavy resistance and were neutralized by the crossfire from French defenses within the harbor. Following this, the Vichy French naval squadron emerged from the harbor to engage the Allied invasion fleet, but these French vessels were ultimately sunk or forced aground.

Captain Frederick Thornton Peters, who led the daring Operation Reservist, received the Victoria Cross for his courageous efforts to carry out the operation amid intense enemy fire in Oran harbor. Over the course of November 8 and 9, there were intense exchanges of artillery between the French shore defenses and the invading forces. The steadfast defense by the French troops in Oran and its vicinities was finally overcome by the heavy shelling from British battleships, leading to Oran's capitulation on November 10.

Operation Torch marked the United States' first significant foray into airborne operations. The 2nd Battalion of the 509th Parachute Infantry Regiment embarked on an ambitious flight from Cornwall, England, traversing over Spain to execute a parachute drop near Oran. Their mission was to seize the Tafraoui and La Sénia airfields, located approximately 15 miles and 5 miles south of Oran, respectively. However, this operation was beset with challenges, particularly issues with communication and navigation. The latter was partly due to HMS Alynbank, the beacon ship, mistakenly broadcasting on an incorrect frequency.

Complications were compounded by adverse weather conditions over Spain and the demanding distance, which led to the dispersal of the formation. This disarray resulted in 30 out of the 37 transport aircraft being forced to make landings on a dry salt lake, significantly west of their intended targets. Out of the remaining planes, one pilot, disoriented, redirected to Gibraltar for landing. Two found their way to French Morocco, while three others mistakenly landed in Spanish Morocco. In one instance, a Dakota mistakenly released its paratroopers over Spanish territory, leading to the internment of 67 American soldiers by Spanish forces until February 1943.

Despite these setbacks, the Tafraoui and La Sénia airfields were ultimately taken. However, due to the myriad of issues that hampered the airborne component of the operation, the contribution of the 2nd Battalion, 509th Parachute Infantry Regiment to the overall success of Operation Torch was relatively minor.

In accordance with the plans formulated in Cherchell, a clandestine operation was executed in Algiers during the early hours of November 8. Led by Henri d'Astier de la Vigerie and José Aboulker, the 400-strong resistance force predominantly composed of Jewish members, known as the Géo Gras Group, initiated a coup in the city. Their operation, which commenced at the stroke of midnight, involved capturing strategic points such as the telephone exchange, radio station, the governor's residence, and the headquarters of the 19th Corps.

Amidst this turmoil, Robert Murphy mobilized a group of men and proceeded to the home of General Alphonse Juin, the foremost French military official in North Africa. Murphy's contingent effectively turned Juin into a hostage as they encircled his residence. Murphy endeavored to convince Juin to ally with the Allied forces. However, an unexpected factor arose: Admiral François Darlan, the commander of all French forces, was incidentally in Algiers on a personal visit. Juin demanded to communicate with Darlan, and despite Murphy's efforts, neither military leader was swayed to join the Allied cause. As the situation unfolded into the morning hours, local law enforcement intervened, resulting in the liberation of both Juin and Darlan.

The Allied invasion known as Operation Torch kicked off on November 8, 1942, with simultaneous landings on three designated beaches near Algiers. Major General Charles W. Ryder, leading the U.S. 34th Infantry Division, commanded the operation on the ground. The British 78th Infantry Division's 11th Brigade Group approached the easternmost beach, the U.S. 168th Regimental Combat Team from the 34th Infantry Division—reinforced by the bulk of the British 1st and 6th Commandos—targeted the central beach, and the U.S. 39th Regimental Combat Team from the 9th Infantry Division, accompanied by the rest of 1 Commando, advanced on the western beach. The British 78th Division's 36th Brigade Group was ready offshore as a floating reserve.

Despite some units mistakenly landing on incorrect beaches, the operation proceeded smoothly due to the unexpectedly low levels of French resistance. French coastal defenses were inoperative, largely due to sabotage efforts by the French Resistance, and one French commander even switched allegiances to the Allies.

The only significant resistance occurred at the Algiers port during Operation Terminal. There, two British destroyers aimed to land U.S. Army Rangers directly onto the docks to prevent the French from destroying vital port infrastructure and scuttling their ships. While heavy artillery fire repelled one destroyer, the other successfully deployed 250 Rangers before being forced to retreat.

The inland advance of the U.S. troops was swift, and by evening, General Juin, the senior French military officer in North Africa, conceded to the Allies, capitulating the city of Algiers by 18:00.

The authority of General Henri Giraud to command French forces proved insufficient as he opted to observe from Gibraltar the outcomes of the ongoing landings. Admiral François Darlan, who was present in Algiers, held the necessary influence. Consequently, General Dwight D. Eisenhower, backed by President Roosevelt and Prime Minister Churchill, entered into an accord with Darlan, appointing him as the French High Commissioner for North Africa. In exchange, on November 10th, Darlan issued commands for all French forces in the region to halt hostilities against Allied troops and to collaborate with them instead. This directive effectively ended French resistance almost immediately, leading to the submission and subsequent integration of the French forces in North Africa into the Allied ranks.

These forces, including a significant number of soldiers from French North Africa, would later contribute significantly to the Allied cause, particularly within the French Expeditionary Corps. By April 1944, the Corps comprised 112,000 troops, with Maghrebis, primarily Moroccans, representing over 60% of its fighters. They would go on to participate valiantly in the Allied campaign in Italy.

Battle of Kasserine Pass

On November 8, 1942, American and British military units made landfalls at various points on the French Morocco and Algerian shores as part of Operation Torch. This operation unfolded shortly after the British Eighth Army, under Lieutenant-General Bernard Montgomery, achieved a decisive victory at the Second Battle of El Alamein. In a countermove, Axis powers hastened to transport German and Italian soldiers from Sicily to Tunisia, a strategically defendable region in North Africa, which was also a mere overnight journey from Sicilian bases. The proximity of Tunisia to Sicily presented a significant challenge to the Allies, as it was nearly impossible for their naval forces to cut off the Axis supply lines, and air strikes were limited by the distance—Tunisia was more than 200 miles from the closest Allied airfield on Malta.

The sequence of events in November and December 1942 to capture Tunis before the Axis could fortify it is known as the Run for Tunis. Hindered by inadequate road and railway links, only a modest Allied force equivalent to a division could be supported in this endeavor. The terrain favored defense, enabling a small number of Axis troops to repel the Allies' advance. Nevertheless, the Allies continued to reinforce their positions, acquire more aircraft, and construct new airfields in eastern Algeria and Tunisia, thereby slowly stifling the Axis influx of reinforcements and supplies to Tunis and Bizerta. Despite these efforts, the Axis had managed to secure a significant military presence in the region.

By January 23, 1943, the Allied Eighth Army had captured Tripoli, a key logistical hub previously under the command of Axis leader Erwin Rommel. Rommel had anticipated this loss and redirected his supply chains to Tunis, seeking to defend the approach to southern Tunisia from Tripoli at Gabès.

Having breached the Atlas Mountains, Allied forces established a forward outpost at Faïd, situated at the eastern foothills, which served as a strategic point. From here, the Allies planned to push eastward to the coast, aiming to separate the Axis contingents in southern Tunisia from those to the north and sever their supply lines to Tunis.

On January 30, units from the 5th Panzer Army, led by General Hans-Jürgen von Arnim, approached the Allied defenses situated at the eastern base of the Atlas Mountains. The French forces encountered the 21st Panzer Division near Faïd, where the French 75 mm guns were effectively employed, inflicting significant losses on the German infantry. Despite this, the German forces easily pushed the defenders back.

The conflict intensified when U.S. artillery and the 1st Armored Division joined in, knocking out a number of enemy tanks and seemingly causing the Germans to retreat hastily. However, this retreat was a ruse; as American forces pursued, they fell into a well-laid ambush by German anti-tank units, suffering substantial losses.

As the 21st Panzer Division pressed its offensive towards Faïd, the American infantry, hindered by their use of shallow shell scrapes for cover instead of deeper foxholes, were vulnerable; German tank drivers exploited this by crushing the scrapes—and the men within—by deliberately driving over them and twisting their tanks. Repeated efforts by the 1st Armored Division to halt the German onslaught proved futile as they discovered each intended defensive position had been preemptively taken by German forces, leading to heavy American casualties.

By February 2, the 1st Armored Division was instructed to cease its offensives and regroup to form a defensive reserve. The German forces had succeeded in capturing the majority of Tunisia and sealing off the gateways to the coastal plains. Although the Allies retained control within the central region of the Atlas Mountains, this position was of limited strategic value since all routes of advance were effectively blocked by the Axis. Over the following two weeks, Rommel and other Axis commanders engaged in deliberations on their next course of action.

Rommel did not initially perceive the Eighth Army to be a considerable threat because, without access to Tripoli, Montgomery's forces in southern Tunisia were limited. It was not until February 9 that ships began to unload supplies there, and it took until the end of the month for Tripoli to become fully functional. In early February, Rommel put forth a plan to the Italian High Command in Rome suggesting an assault with two battlegroups, which would include elements from the 5th Panzer Army, aimed at American supply depots located west of the Atlas Mountains in Algeria. His strategy aimed to seize these depots and disrupt American efforts to gather forces near Tebessa. However, Arnim had reservations, and this led to a week's delay until an agreement was reached on initiating Operation Frühlingswind—where the 5th Panzer Army would strike at the American communications and supply hub at Sidi Bou Zid. Concurrently, Rommel's units, stationed about 60 miles to the southwest, were set to execute Operation Morgenluft with the goal of capturing Gafsa and pushing towards Tozeur.

The assault began on February 14, with the 10th and 21st Panzer divisions launching the Battle of Sidi Bou Zid, approximately 10 miles west of Faïd, on the inland plains of the Atlas Mountains. The American armored forces were overpowered, and their infantry, positioned on three hills without inter-supporting capabilities, became encircled. A subsequent counterattack on the following day was easily thwarted, leading to the German advance toward Sbeitla on February 16.

After the victory at Sidi Bou Zid, Rommel directed the Afrika Korps Assault Group to strike Gafsa on February 15. Anticipating this move, General Anderson commanded the retreat from Gafsa the night prior, choosing to establish a stronger defensive line in the surrounding hills of Feriana. Confronted by the risk to the southern flank, Anderson, with Eisenhower's concurrence, commanded a withdrawal to the Western Dorsale, stretching from Feriana northward.

By the early hours of February 17, General Fredendall had ordered a pullback from Sbeitla and Feriana. This allowed the U.S. II Corps to regroup at the Kasserine and Sbiba Passes on the western side of the Atlas range. The cost was high for the U.S. forces, incurring losses of 2,546 personnel, 103 tanks, 280 vehicles, 18 field guns, 3 anti-tank guns, and an anti-aircraft battery.

Amid Axis control of all Tunisian territory, strategists debated the next move as they awaited the arrival of the Eighth Army at Mareth. Rommel advocated for an aggressive maneuver. His plan was to exploit the Kasserine Pass to strike the heart of the U.S. II Corps stationed at Tébessa. He aimed to seize U.S. supplies within Algeria, diminish Allied capacity to assault the coastal route connecting Mareth to Tunis, and jeopardize the southern flank of the First Army. Rommel presented his strategy to Albert Kesselring, who endorsed it and passed it along with his support to the Italian High Command in Rome.

On the afternoon of February 19, Rommel got the green light from Comando Supremo for a modified version of his proposal. He would command the 10th and 21st Panzer Divisions, repositioned from Arnim's 5th Panzer Army, to press through the Kasserine and Sbiba passes towards Thala and Le Kef to the north, with an objective to clear the Western Dorsale and put pressure on the 1st Army's flank.

However, the revised plan dismayed Rommel, as it would spread out his forces and leave them vulnerable through the mountain passes. Rommel saw a more focused thrust at Tébessa as a calculated gamble that could significantly disrupt Allied operational capabilities in central Tunisia and capture the strategic airfield at Youks-les-Bains, just west of Tébessa, along with much-needed supplies.

Before dawn on February 19, Rommel directed the Afrika Korps Assault Group stationed at Feriana to launch an offensive on the Kasserine Pass. Concurrently, he commanded the 21st Panzer Division, located at Sbeitla, to initiate a northward push through the pass that branched eastward to Sbiba and Ksour. Furthermore, the Kampfgruppe von Broich—a battlegroup detached by Arnim from the 10th Panzer Division—was ordered to gather at Sbeitla, positioning it to capitalize on any breakthroughs achieved at either pass.

In the vicinity of Sbiba, the German forces, consisting of Battle Groups Stenkhoff and Schuette and what remained of the 21st Panzer Division, launched an assault. Opposing the German armored units was the British 6th Armoured Division, which was without the 26th Armoured Brigade except for the tanks of the 16/5th Lancers that had been redeployed to Thala. Alongside the British were the American 18th Regimental Combat Team from the 1st Infantry Division and three battalions of infantry from the 34th Infantry Division. Support included three U.S. Field Artillery battalions, elements of two British anti-tank regiments, and some French units. The defense was robust, fortified by combined arms firepower and minefields laid across the German path of advance. This cohesive defensive stand successfully halted the 21st Panzer Division's progress, eventually forcing a retreat by February 20.

The Kasserine Pass was defended by an array of Allied forces: the U.S. 1st Battalion from the 26th Regimental Combat Team, the U.S. 19th Combat Engineer Regiment, the 6th Field Artillery Battalion, a battalion equipped with tank destroyers, and a unit of French artillery. To their west was French General Welvert's Task Force Welvert, which included a U.S. Ranger battalion, a U.S. infantry battalion, three French infantry battalions, two U.S. field artillery battalions, four French artillery batteries, and various engineer and anti-aircraft elements. Further west, blocking the route from Feriana to Tebessa, was Task Force Bowen, composed of the 3rd Battalion of the 26th Regimental Combat Team. To the north, near Tebessa, the reorganizing 1st Armored Division was stationed, though only its Combat Command B was battle-ready.

On the night of February 18, Colonel Alexander Stark, commander of the 26th RCT, was charged with the defense of the pass and the assembled units were designated Stark Force.

An early assault by the 33rd Reconnaissance Unit to catch the Kasserine defenses off-guard was unsuccessful. In response, a battalion of Panzer grenadiers advanced into the valley and another scaled the eastern hill, Djebel Semmama, making only modest gains under heavy artillery fire. The 1/8th Panzer Regiment sent tanks into battle by midday, but they achieved little against the resolute defense.

Rommel planned for a more forceful offensive the next morning, directing units from the 10th Panzer Division to join the Kasserine assault in conjunction with the Afrika Korps Assault Group, supported by parts of the Italian 131st Armored Division Centauro.

Meanwhile, British forces from the 26th Armoured Brigade of the 6th Armoured Division had been gathering at Thala. Brigadier Dunphie, upon conducting forward reconnaissance, opted to engage, although the First Army headquarters limited him to deploying Gore Force, a modest task group consisting of an infantry company, a squadron with 11 tanks, an artillery battery, and an anti-tank troop. Brigadier Cameron Nicholson of the 6th Armoured Division was appointed to lead Nickforce, which commanded all units positioned northwest of the pass.

Overnight, the American units holding the commanding heights on either side of the Kasserine Pass were overwhelmed. By 8:30 am the next day, German panzer grenadiers, alongside Italian Bersaglieri, renewed their offensive. By 10:00 am, Brigadier Dunphie perceived Stark Force was on the brink of collapse and dispatched Gore Force to bolster the defenses near Thala. Concurrently, elements of the Italian Centauro Division initiated their onslaught towards Tebessa, pressing their attack throughout the afternoon.

On the morning of February 20, during the initial assault on the strategic town of Djebel, the 5th Bersaglieri Regiment launched a direct offensive against the American positions. The intense battle raged on until they breached the defenses, albeit with the loss of their regimental leader, Colonel Bonfatti. This breakthrough was pivotal, clearing the path towards Thala and Tebessa. By noon, the tide had turned decisively as Axis armored forces surged through the pass, inflicting a severe defeat on the retreating U.S. forces, including the 1st U.S. Armored Division.

The Italian regiment's efforts were particularly noted for their significance in the Axis triumph, receiving high praise from General Bülowius, the commander of the DAK assault group. At 1:00 pm, Rommel directed two battalions from the 10th Panzer Division to join the attack, effectively overcoming the remaining defenses.

Tanks and Bersaglieri from the Centauro Division, advancing along Highway 13, overwhelmed the 19th Combat Engineer Regiment. The beleaguered U.S. troops fell back in disarray toward Djebel el Hamra, where Combat Command B of the 1st Armored Division was making its approach. Along the route to Thala, Gore Force fought a rearguard action, retreating in stages and sacrificing all of its tanks before finally regrouping with the 26th Armoured Brigade, located about 10 miles rearward.

On the afternoon of February 21, the Afrika Korps Assault Group progressed along the Hatab River valley, aiming for Haidra and Tebessa, only to encounter sturdy resistance at Djebel el Hamra from the U.S. 16th Infantry Regiment of the 1st Infantry Division, along with Combat Command B of the 1st Armored Division. The combined German and Italian advance stalled against the steadfast American defense, even under the strain of persistent aerial bombardment and ground assaults.

With the Axis push towards Tebessa effectively checked, American commanders General Paul Robinett and General Terry Allen focused on orchestrating a counteroffensive scheduled for February 22. However, the dynamic nature of the battlefield led to disrupted plans on both sides. In a renewed attack on the morning of February 22, Axis forces—including the 5th Bersaglieri, a Semovente detachment from the Centauro Division, and the 15th Panzer Division—mounted a fresh offensive towards Bou Chebka Pass.

Despite the intensity of the Axis assault, the American defense lines withstood the pressure. By the afternoon, U.S. infantry and armor units initiated a powerful counterattack, reversing the gains of the German-Italian coalition. The momentum shifted as over 400 Axis soldiers were captured, and the American forces pushed their advantage deep into the Afrika Korps' positions.

Rommel accompanied the principal elements of the 10th Panzer Division as they advanced toward Thala. There, the 26th Armoured Brigade, together with what remained of the U.S. 26th Infantry Regiment, had established defensive positions on the ridges. The town's fall and the severance of the southern route from Thala to Tebessa would isolate the U.S. 9th Infantry Division to the north and entrap Combat Command B of the 1st Armored Division between the 10th Panzer and its support units that were advancing northward on the second road toward Tebessa. The defending Allies executed a stubborn, costly withdrawal in front of Thala, relinquishing one ridge after another until, by nightfall, they had managed to halt the German advance just short of the town.

During the night, the artillery of the 9th Infantry Division, which had traveled a grueling 800 miles from Morocco since February 17, established their positions. By the following day, the frontline was primarily manned by British infantry, with strong artillery support consolidated under Brigadier General Stafford LeRoy Irwin, the American artillery commander. This force included 36 British guns, armoured cars from the Derbyshire Yeomanry, and tanks from the 17th/21st Lancers.

General Anderson had directed the 9th Infantry Division and its artillery to relocate to Le Kef in anticipation of a German assault. However, Major General Ernest N. Harmon, dispatched by Eisenhower to evaluate the situation, countermanded the movement, instructing the 9th Division's artillery to remain in position. On the morning of February 22, a heavy artillery barrage from the massed Allied guns pre-empted any further attacks by the 10th Panzer Division, causing substantial damage to their armor and logistical support and throwing their communication lines into disarray. The battle group leader, Broich, opted to hold his position to regroup. Nevertheless, as Allied reinforcements poured in, the 10th Panzer was subjected to relentless bombardment and was compelled to retreat under cover of darkness, withdrawing from the field of battle.

Stretched too thin and facing dwindling supplies, with their forces pinned by overwhelming Allied artillery at Thala and now under counterattack from U.S. forces along the Hatab River, Rommel acknowledged that his forces were exhausted. The concerted attempts by German and Italian units at Sbiba, along the Hatab River, and at Thala had not yielded the decisive breakthrough in the Allied defense that he had hoped for. Recognizing the slim chance of turning the tide, Rommel considered it more strategic to consolidate his forces in southern Tunisia to potentially outmaneuver the Eighth Army, which was still consolidating its formations. Despite the setbacks, Rommel could take solace in having inflicted considerable losses on the Allies and having dismantled their formations around Gafsa and Sbeitla.

At a strategic conference at Rommel's headquarters in Kasserine on February 23, Field Marshal Albert Kesselring and his Chief of Staff, Siegfried Westphal, urged Rommel to reconsider, believing opportunities for success remained. However, Rommel's conviction was unshakable; Kesselring ultimately concurred, and that evening, orders from the Italian High Command in Rome called for a cessation of the offensive and a withdrawal of all Axis units to their initial positions.

The retreat of the Axis forces was accelerated by a formidable aerial assault from the Americans on the pass on February 23. By the evening of February 24, the Allies had reclaimed the pass. Feriana fell back into Allied control, with Sidi Bou Zid and Sbeitla being recaptured shortly thereafter.

Milton Keynes UK
Ingram Content Group UK Ltd.
UKHW020654271123
433341UK00021B/1890